Group Interventions for Children
with Autism Spectrum Disorders

Group Interventions for Children with Autism Spectrum Disorders

A Focus on Social Competency and Social Skills

Albert J. Cotugno

Jessica Kingsley Publishers
London and Philadelphia

First published in 2009
by Jessica Kingsley Publishers
116 Pentonville Road
London N1 9JB, UK
and
400 Market Street, Suite 400
Philadelphia, PA 19106, USA

www.jkp.com

Copyright © Albert J. Cotugno 2009

Library of Congress Cataloging in Publication Data
Cotugno, Albert J.
 Group interventions for children with autism spectrum disorders : a focus on social competency and
  social skills / Albert J. Cotugno.
   p. cm.
 Includes bibliographical references and index.
 ISBN 978-1-84310-910-5 (pb : alk. paper) 1. Autism in children. 2. Group psychotherapy for children.
  I. Title.
 RJ506.A9C68 2009
 618.92'89152--dc22

                                        2008055641

British Library Cataloguing in Publication Data
A CIP catalogue record for this book is available from the British Library

ISBN 978 1 84310 910 5

Printed and bound in Great Britain by
Athenaeum Press, Gateshead, Tyne and Wear

Contents

List of Figures

Acknowledgements

Our doubts are traitors
And make us lose the good we oft might win
By fearing to attempt.

Measure for Measure,
William Shakespeare, 1604

Writing this book has truly been a labor of love. It was however, not completed in a vacuum and because of that, there are many to thank. To those friends and colleagues who provided consistent support and encouragement, I am most grateful, especially to Peter Szuch who kept me from taking anything too seriously; to Michael Cauley for being in the right place at the right time; to Scott McLeod whose steady leadership of YouthCare has allowed it to thrive; and to those teachers and mentors of whom there are too many to name.

Most importantly, this work would not be possible without the constant support and presence of my spouse, Debra Levine, the most gifted and talented special educator I know; my children, Rebecca, a thinker of meaning and purpose, and David, a sensitive soul and a born teacher; and finally, my father, who gives me loyalty, intensity, and perseverance, and my late mother whose compassion, love of knowledge, learning, and values, live on in the hearts of those left behind.

Preface

Autism Spectrum Disorders (ASD) refers to a group of developmental disorders appearing in children soon after birth. They are characterized by significant and pervasive impairments in critical areas of development including language and communication skills, typical behavioral skills and interactions, and social interactive abilities. Some children may be impaired in only a single area while others may exhibit problems across a broad range of development. The number of areas of impairments and the severity of the delay in any area combine to provide differentiation of the nature of the disorder within the individual and from individual to individual and allow for categorization and diagnosis where appropriate. The study of ASD is a fast growing and rapidly evolving field and this has paralleled a marked increase in the number of individuals being diagnosed with ASD. Currently, the Centers for Disease Control and Prevention (2007) report that in studies of broad cohorts of eight-year-old children across the United States, combined data indicate that 1 in 150 children are currently being diagnosed with some form of ASD.

The intent of this book is to provide a context and a model for understanding ASD and an approach to addressing and managing some of the prominent issues that interfere with social interactions and communications. Part I places a frame around ASD, with an understanding of its historical context and how and why terms are defined and used in specific ways, followed by a discussion and understanding of the social aspects of the disorders, including the relationship of typical social development to these disorders. Part II addresses issues related to the description, management, and treatment of core deficits (referred to here as key variables or processes) as they occur in social interactions and social situations. Finally, and most importantly, Part III provides a description of a model for group interventions with ASD individuals which is grounded within a stage-based, cognitive-developmental approach and which makes maximum use of peer interactions, group therapeutic principles, cognitive-behavioral techniques, and direct skill instruction. This approach is a peer group-based, interactive, therapeutic process aimed at developing and enhancing social interactive and social communicative structures and skills of ASD individuals believed necessary for growth and progress within a social world.

PART I

AUTISM SPECTRUM DISORDERS (ASD)

Do not be anxious about tomorrow,
For tomorrow will be anxious for itself.

Matthew, 6:34

Part I provides a brief introduction to ASD and how it relates to the approach described in this book. Current definitions are presented in order to understand the range of thinking (and controversy) that continues to exist and influence the field as intervention models are sought.

Next a broad historical perspective is presented to trace and to understand the path that ASD diagnoses have traveled and how we have arrived at our current state of understanding. Additional definitions of ASD are also briefly presented to provide the broadest understanding of the diagnostic issues that are currently being addressed.

Last in Part I, since ASD is primarily a social disorder for many individuals on the spectrum, an understanding of social development is considered critical, particularly as it relates to the treatment and management of the social deficits observed in ASD individuals. Social development as it relates to both typical and ASD individuals is described and later considered within the group-focused, peer-based, cognitive-developmental stage model described in this book.

Chapter 1

Introduction

Autism Spectrum Disorders (ASD) are a group of neurologically-based disorders which significantly affect development in social, behavioral, and language/communication areas. ASD includes the diagnoses of Autistic Disorder (AuD), Asperger's Disorder (AD), and Pervasive Developmental Disorder-Not Otherwise Specified (PDD-NOS) and are considered to be part of the global category of Pervasive Developmental Disorders (PDD), due to their extensive, pervasive, and debilitating effects on the particular areas affected. At this time, the causes of these disorders are unknown and there are no known preventions or "cures." Categorization and often diagnosis of ASD individuals is complicated by differences in specific symptom clusters as manifested from individual to individual, in the range and intensity of these symptoms, and in the degree of impairment that these symptoms cause for the individual. Accurate and consistent diagnosis is further complicated by ongoing controversy within the ASD field about what specific criteria constitute a given ASD diagnosis, where the borders and boundaries of ASD diagnoses lie, and how best to construct research and studies to address these issues. Nevertheless, great strides have been made in understanding these disorders and effective interventions which lessen and diminish their intensity and improve their outcome continue to be developed and tested. Still, developing, assessing, and implementing promising interventions continue to be a time consuming and painstaking process requiring many years and many dedicated individuals. Yet as Wing 1991 (p.116) states:

> the best way to help any socially impaired child is to recognize the social impairment, examine for and, as far as possible, treat or alleviate any identifiable underlying cause or associated conditions, assess specific skills and disabilities and overall level of intelligence, then use this information to plan an individual programme.

Individuals with ASD exhibit a wide range of behaviors, often with significant variability from individual to individual. While impairments in social interaction, communication, and repetitive and perseverative behaviors, may be most obvious and prominent, other behaviors may be more subtle and variable. Individuals with ASD typically also have difficulties in one or more of the following areas: perseverative thoughts, persistent preoccupations; narrow, overfocused interests; high needs for routines and sameness; inflexibility and rigidity; poor anxiety management; poor perspective-taking and theory of mind; clumsiness or poor fine or gross motor skills; sensory issues; attention problems; or inability to read or interpret nonverbal, social cues.

In this book, specific aspects of ASD are addressed, focusing primarily on significant impairments in social interaction, including an inability to understand and interpret nonverbal behaviors in others, a failure to develop age-appropriate peer relationships, a lack of interest or enjoyment in social interactions, and a lack of social or emotional reciprocity. In addition, there is also a focus on those concerns characterized by the presence of repetitive and stereotypic patterns of behavior, interests, or activities, including intense and persistent preoccupations, a rigid or inflexible adherence to rituals or routines, and repetitive, stereotypic motor mannerisms.

The approach described here targets those ASD individuals who exhibit social impairments, but without marked cognitive or communication deficits. In the literature, particularly the *Diagnostic and Statistical Manual – Fourth Edition* (DSM IV) (American Psychiatric Association 1994), this description of ASD is viewed as describing primarily individuals with Asperger's Disorder (AD). Many AD individuals may benefit from this approach, but by definition, other individuals with disorders such as High Functioning Autism (HFA), PDD-NOS, and AuD, may also be included when appropriate.

This book focuses on individuals with ASD who function at the higher end of the ASD spectrum, which generally refers to those individuals with average or better cognitive abilities, no significant communication deficits, manageable behavior, and no significant mental illness. While this group is broad and diagnostically complex, they share many characteristics and behaviors that can be addressed with the program and treatment interventions described here. The common trait for those ASD individuals which provides the primary emphasis for this book is the basic inability to relate to and engage consistently in age-appropriate social interactions, particularly with peers. These individuals appear to lack the basic social competence for the development of effective and successful interpersonal relationships with peers and significant adults. For example, many ASD individuals may be quite oblivious to the social situation they may be in, others may recognize the social needs of the situation but not know what to do about it, while others may recognize the needs of the situation and make attempts to engage, but be totally lacking the specific skills necessary to effectively complete the social exchange.

This book first considers definitions of ASD, then describes historical and background information. This is followed by a discussion of social development in typical and ASD individuals with emphasis on key variables known to be deficient in ASD individuals. This sets the foundation for a description of a group-based intervention program. This program places primary focus on a stage-based model within a cognitive-developmental framework and uses group therapy principles, cognitive-behavioral approaches, and skill-based instruction, to treat high functioning individuals with ASD. A guiding principle in this program is characterized as a Process/Skill approach, that is, the process or structure (referred to here in social development as social competency) must first be in place and be available to the individual so that subsequent skill learning (referred to here in social development as social skills) can take place.

For all individuals, the development of social competence depends on the interaction of inherent genetic and temperament characteristics, aspects of biological, physiological, cognitive, neurological, behavioral, and emotional development, and social experiences. In typical development, social competence consists of several different aspects of social development, including the ability to recognize and understand a social situation, the ability to initiate a social interchange, the ability to understand its content and move it forward, and the ability to respond to the range of stimuli available from both other individuals involved and specific aspects of the situation or environment (i.e., engage in and follow a discussion or play activity in an appropriate setting). In essence, social competence is the capacity to engage in a reciprocal process of shared experience with another individual or individuals (Shores 1987) while communicating on many verbal and nonverbal levels and understanding context, situation, and environment. While extremely complex in nature, this process includes the capacity to attain and maintain developmentally appropriate levels of social recognition and awareness, social interest and motivation, social comprehension, memory, learning, social skill development, and social-emotional affective states (e.g., sympathy, empathy). Social competence is the result of ever changing and evolving experiences across a wide range of development affecting one's capacities to understand and to interact with other human beings.

While social competence relates to the ability or capacity to engage successfully in social interaction, social skills on the other hand, are the actual tools or skills that enable the social interaction itself to proceed and to work smoothly. Social skills are the actual ways an individual uses to initiate, to engage, to communicate, and to respond to others when involved in an interchange. In other words, social competence is the ability and capacity to engage in a reciprocal social interchange (consisting of the underlying structure necessary to recognize, acknowledge, engage, and follow through in the situation), while social skills provide the actual ways in which the individual performs in this situation (e.g., makes eye contact, says hello, asks a question, listens and formulates a response, arranges a subsequent meeting, says goodbye).

Some ASD individuals lack many or all aspects of social competence, some possess few or no social skills, and many struggle with a variety and range of combinations of social competence and social skill deficits. The approach described here attempts to systematically assess the ASD individual's social abilities and skills and to thoughtfully place them in a social situation (i.e., small group, peer-based, structure based, skill-focused, and adult-monitored situation) where the individual's social competence and social skills needs can be addressed. While ASD individuals may benefit from a variety of different types of interventions (Klin and Volkmar 2000), it is believed that the core deficit in social interaction can be best addressed by focusing both on social competency and social skill development within a group setting with peers and monitored as needed by adults. This setting provides the environment for learning about and understanding the process of reciprocal social interchange and learning the skills needed to engage others successfully while at the same time experiencing relationships, connections, and emotional experiences as part of a therapeutic group environment.

In this environment, related to both the individual within the group and the group as a whole, a cognitive-developmental model is adhered to at each point in time. Development is viewed as experiencing and learning through stages and within each stage of development, building systematically an understanding of the individual's own and the group's capacities and abilities to engage, then teaching the relevant skills to effectively and in age-appropriate ways interact with peers in natural settings. This book will describe the group model developed which operates within a cognitive-developmental framework and which makes use of group therapy principles, peer-based interactions, structured cognitive-behavioral techniques, and skill-based instruction.

Chapter 2

Definitions of Autism Spectrum Disorders (ASD) and Pervasive Developmental Disorders (PDD)

Autism Spectrum Disorders (ASD) are considered to be neurologically-based disorders of unknown origin which have gained the increasing attention and interest of professionals recently. Particularly over the past decade, dramatic increases in the incidence of ASD have been reported with most recent estimates ranging as high as 1 in 150 (Centers for Disease Control and Prevention 2007) and as high as 1 in 210 for children with Asperger's Disorder (AD) (Ehlers and Gillberg 1993; Kadesjo, Gillberg, and Hagberg 1999). Overall, prevalence reports range from 0.3 to as high as 70 per 10,000 children (Fombonne 2003) and on average, reflect a nearly 1300 percent increase over a ten-year span (1992–2002) of children classified with ASD who receive special education services (Center for Environmental Health, Environmental Epidemiology Program 2005). However, ongoing controversy about the most appropriate diagnostic criteria for Pervasive Developmental Disorders (PDD), ASD, and AD and how they are applied in both research and clinical settings, may have contributed to differences in prevalence estimates and to the application of consistent, appropriate, and valid diagnostic criteria. Other factors, such as an increased awareness in the general public, earlier and more thorough diagnosis, increased responsibilities shifted to educational settings, an increased number of professionals in the field, increased parental involvement, and aggressive advocacy, may also be contributing to increased prevalence rates.

Within the *Diagnostic and Statistical Manual of Mental Disorders, Fourth Edition* (DSM IV) (American Psychiatric Association 1994), the most widely used manual for diagnostic classification, particularly within the United States, the diagnostic category of PDD contains disorders characterized and defined by severe, serious, and pervasive impairments in several areas of development, including reciprocal social interaction skills, language and communication skills, or the presence of restricted, stereotypic, repetitive behavior, interests, or activities, providing sharp and marked contrast from the appropriate development in these areas by normally developing individuals. The DSM IV category of PDD includes Autistic Disorder (AuD), Asperger's Disorder (AD), Pervasive Developmental Disorder-Not Otherwise Specified (PDD-NOS), Rett's Disorder, and Childhood Disintegrative Disorder (CDD).

Rett's Disorder and CDD however, are both disorders associated with progressive loss of functioning and of skills that had previously been attained within the first few years of life as well as with severe mental retardation. Both are low incidence, rarely seen disorders, with Rett's Disorder known to occur only in females. While both are of unknown origin, each appears to have strong neurological and genetic components and the appropriateness of their placement within the PDD category remains controversial. While currently included as PDD, neither Rett's Disorder nor CDD are considered part of the autism spectrum.

Autism Spectrum Disorders are considered a subcategory of PDD, and include only AuD, AD, and PDD-NOS. These three diagnoses constitute the "autism spectrum" with AuD at one end, and including lower functioning individuals, and AS at the other end, including higher functioning individuals. PPD-NOS appears to fall somewhere in the middle. In addition, each diagnosis itself also appears to operate within a continuum or range of functioning with lower functioning individuals at one end and higher functioning individuals at the other end.

Figure 2.1 Pervasive Developmental Disorders (PDD) and Autism Spectrum Disorders (ASD)

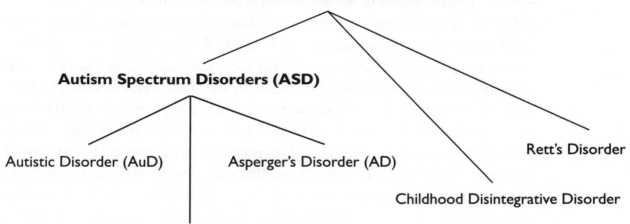

Autistic Disorder (AuD)

Autistic Disorder is a term used to describe individuals who demonstrate marked impairment or abnormal development in the three areas of social interaction, communication (functional and/or pragmatic), and range of activities and interests (i.e., restrictive, stereotypical, repetitive, self-destructive). Approximately 75 percent of AuD individuals appear to function in the mentally retarded range, while 25 percent appear to be functioning at average or higher levels. Thus at one end of the AuD continuum would be individuals with significant social interaction problems, significant communication or language delays, and restricted, repetitive, and stereotyped patterns and who may also experience significant, even profound cognitive, deficiencies. At the higher end of the AuD continuum would be individuals with less significant social interaction difficulties (e.g., possibly meeting only two of four DSM IV criteria), less severe communication delays (e.g., possibly meeting only one of four criteria), and fewer or less intense restricted, repetitive, or stereotyped behaviors (e.g., possibly meeting only one of four criteria), and who may not possess any delays in cognitive functioning. In DSM IV, AuD is defined by twelve criteria, four each within the categories of social interaction, communication, and repetitive and stereotyped patterns of behavior, interests, and activities. To obtain a diagnosis of AuD, an individual must meet criteria on a total of at least six items. These six criteria must include at least two problems from the category of social impairment. Impairments in social interaction are defined by: difficulties with nonverbal behaviors such as eye-to-eye gaze, facial expression, body postures, and gestures to regulate social interaction; difficulties with developmentally appropriate peer relationships; an inability to spontaneously seek or share enjoyment, interests, or achievements with other people; and problems with social or emotional reciprocity.

These six criteria must include at least one deficiency from the category of communication. Deficits in communication are defined by: the absence or significant delay in the development of spoken language; significant difficulty in initiating or sustaining conversation; stereotypic, repetitive, or idiosyncratic language usage; and the absence of developmentally appropriate spontaneous pretend or social imitative play.

Finally in meeting the minimum of six criteria necessary for a diagnosis of AuD, at least one deficiency must be present from the category of restricted, repetitive and stereotyped patterns of behavior, interests, and activities. These deficiencies include: an intense and overwhelming focus or preoccupation with one or more stereotyped and restricted patterns of interest; an inflexible adherence to routines or rituals; stereotyped and repetitive motor mannerisms; and persistent focus or preoccupations with parts of objects. In addition, delayed or abnormal functioning must have been demonstrated by the individual in at least one of these three categories (social interaction, communication, or symbolic, imaginative play) prior to the age of three.

Those individuals diagnosed with AuD who are capable of functioning cognitively and intellectually at average or higher levels are often described with High Functioning Autism (HFA) (DeMyer, Hingtgen and Jackson 1981). While HFA is not a diagnostic category in itself, it serves to help differentiate levels of functioning within AuD. However, the term also creates confusion in places where there appears to be overlap of HFA/AuD and AD.

Asperger's Disorder (AD)

Within DSM IV, AD is classified within the broad domain of PDD and is considered one of the ASD which involve individuals functioning at the higher end of the spectrum and generally with higher levels of competency in all of the key areas of functioning (social interaction, language/communication, patterns of behavior). While AD is considered as part of the autism spectrum, it meets only two of three main AuD categories, those including impairment in social interaction and the development of restrictive or repetitive patterns of behavior, interests, and activities. It is considered "milder" relative to AuD.

In AD, there is typically no indication of functional language impairment (e.g., mechanics), although pragmatic language may be deficient, and there are no indications of significantly impaired intelligence or cognition. AD is thus considered to exist at the high end of the spectrum with profound, low functioning autistic individuals at one end and with bright, verbal, often high achieving AD individuals at the other end (Wing 1988). In DSM IV, an AD diagnosis would apply only if the criteria of other PDD are not met. Most often this requires assessing the onset and presence of any specific communication or language deficits and whether this then requires consideration within the category of AuD. In DSM IV, AD is defined by eight criteria, four each within the categories of social interaction and of restricted repetitive, and stereotyped patterns of behavior, interests, and activities. To obtain a diagnosis of AD, an individual must meet criteria on a total of at least three of the six criteria. These six criteria must include at least two problems from the category of social impairment. Impairments in social interaction are defined by: difficulties with nonverbal behaviors such as eye-to-eye gaze, facial expression, body postures, and gestures to regulate social interaction; difficulties with developmentally appropriate peer relationships; an inability to spontaneously seek or share enjoyment, interests, or achievements with other people; and problems with social or emotional reciprocity.

In meeting the minimum of six criteria necessary for a diagnosis of AD, at least one deficiency must be present from the category of restricted, repetitive and stereotyped patterns of behavior, interests, and activities. These deficiencies include: an intense and overwhelming focus or preoccupation with one or more stereotyped and restricted patterns of interest; an inflexible adherence to routines or rituals; stereotyped and repetitive motor mannerisms; and persistent focus or preoccupations with parts of objects. These must cause clinically significant impairment in social, occupational, or other important areas of functioning.

Pervasive Developmental Disorder-Not Otherwise Specified (PDD-NOS)

When full criteria is not met for one of the specific PDD, but there is significant and pervasive impairment in one or more of the areas of social interaction, communication, or restrictive, stereotypic patterns of behavior, then a default category of PDD-NOS, may be applied.

In DSM IV, PDD-NOS is defined as severe and pervasive impairment in one or more of the three areas of social interaction, communication, and restricted repetitive, and stereotyped patterns of behavior, interests, and activities. To obtain a diagnosis of PDD-NOS, an individual must meet criteria in *one or more* areas which include social interaction (at least two of the four criteria), communication (at least one of the four criteria), or restricted repetitive, and stereotyped patterns of behavior, interests, and activities (at least one of the four criteria), but the individual must not meet criteria for another specific PDD (e.g., AuD, AD).

PDD-NOS remains a somewhat ambiguous category used for individuals who do not clearly fit into any other PDD category. PDD-NOS is also likely to span the entire spectrum, depending on the number and severity and extent of impairments.

Since the approach described in this book places primary emphasis on impairments in social interaction, individuals with PDD-NOS are included only if there is significant impairment in social interaction or social interchange with generally adequate cognitive abilities. By definition, all AD individuals would be considered appropriate for this approach given the absence of language or communication deficits, but the presence of impairments in social interaction with restricted, stereotypic, and repetitive thoughts or behaviors. Individuals with AuD would be included only if they have adequate communication skills and function at a high level, typically characterizing these AuD individuals as HFA. To best use this group-focused approach, basic functional language and communication skills are necessary and considered in the group placement process.

While there is general consensus around the definition of AuD, there is more confusion and controversy around other ASD, such as AD and PDD-NOS, as well as the grey areas where the PDD overlap. For example, several definitions have been developed and used by different researchers in the study of AD. Volkmar *et al.* (2004) identified at least five different definitions for AD currently in use. Nevertheless, the most widely used criteria continue to be the DSM IV and *International Classification of Diseases, 10th Edition* (ICD-10) (World Health Organization 1993). However, since multiple definitions have remained in use, this confusion and controversy remains centered upon the most appropriate diagnostic criteria and where these criteria overlap and intersect with AuD. Most importantly, this in turn has clouded research attempts and outcomes.

Chapter 3

Historical Background for ASD

Early developments

Early in the twentieth century, much work in the psychiatric and psychological worlds focused on understanding and refining diagnostic and nomenclature systems. Most of this work was directed toward adults with little attention paid to children. These attempts at defining and classifying mental disorders were an important part of understanding the rapidly changing worlds of the late nineteenth and early twentieth century. During this time, the psychoanalytic theories of Sigmund Freud were stirring great interest and controversy in Europe, the behaviorist approaches of John Watson were growing in popularity in America, and a wide range of alternative approaches to treating serious mental disorders in both adults and children were emerging and being explored.

In 1908, a Swiss psychiatrist, Eugen Bleuler, introduced the term schizophrenia to describe the disorder he was observing and to differentiate it from what had been previously known as dementia praecox, a name given by Emil Kraeplin. Bleuler described schizophrenia as an associative disturbance, characterized by the splitting of different psychic functions. He also introduced two additional concepts to explain schizophrenia; ambivalence, the ability for mutually exclusive contradictions to exist side by side within the psyche, and autism, a detachment and loss of contact with reality, "a withdrawal of the patient to his fantasies, against which any influence from outside becomes an intolerable disturbance" (Bleuler 1951). Bleuler's descriptions of schizophrenic disorders provided a foundation for understanding serious mental disorders in the first half of the twentieth century.

Bleuler used the term autism as a way of describing a specific type of social withdrawal that he observed in schizophrenia, that is, a near complete withdrawal from social interaction and relationships and a turning in to oneself to the exclusion of the world around oneself. Both Leo Kanner and Hans Asperger would later reference Bleuler's work and "borrow" his use of the term autism as they applied it to their own work.

Although Bleuler worked primarily with adults, his descriptions of schizophrenic disorders were also applied to children by others (Bender 1952; Caplan 1955; Mahler 1952). The term "childhood schizophrenia" became increasingly prevalent, emphasizing withdrawal and detachment and viewing these issues as related to a mental (i.e., emotional) disorder similar to adult forms of psychosis and schizophrenia. At that time, the term autism was being used primarily to describe the process of withdrawal and detachment observed and a collection of symptoms related to it, specific to particular types of serious mental disorders. For a significant amount of time, the terms childhood schizophrenia and early infantile autism were used interchangeably, as it was the appearance of significant withdrawal and detachment from the real world that were viewed as hallmarks of serious infantile and childhood disturbance. They were viewed primarily as a function of a mental (i.e., emotional) disorder which at the time were considered to have their origins in factors related to constitutional, familial, and environmental breakdowns. In Bleuler's move away from viewing mental illness as organically based, the explanations of cause were directed back to the individual, family, or determining situation or environment. The work of others (i.e., Freud, Watson) was supportive of these positions.

Figure 3.1 Significant developments in the history of Autism Spectrum Disorders (ASD)

1908	Eugen Bleuler	Introduces the term schizophrenia, which he describes using the concepts of ambivalence and autism
1938	Hans Asperger	Publishes first paper describing "autistic psychopathy" observed at Children's Hospital in Vienna
1943	Leo Kanner	Publishes paper describing eleven boys with "disturbances of affective contact" at Johns Hopkins in Baltimore
1944	Hans Asperger	Publishes paper extensively describing "autistic psychopathy" in four boys observed at Children's Hospital in Vienna
1978	ICD-9	World Health Organization officially lists Infantile Autism as a diagnosis in the *International Classification of Disease 9th Edition* diagnostic manual
1980	Hans Asperger	Dies October 21
1980	DSM III	Infantile Autism included for first time in DSM within a new category of Pervasive Developmental Disorders (PDD), distinct from psychotic disorders
1981	Leo Kanner	Dies April 4
1981	Lorna Wing	Uses the term Asperger's Syndrome for first time, considering it one of several entities within ASD
1981	DeMyer, Hingtgen,& Jackson	Use of the term High Functioning Autism (HFA) for the first time
1987	DSM III-R	Infantile Autism diagnostic label changed to Autistic Disorder (AuD)
1988	London	First international conference on Asperger Syndrome held
1988	Lorna Wing	Uses the term autistic continuum to define the range of possible autism disorders, ranging from profound to mild
1989	Christopher Gillberg	Publishes a set of diagnostic criteria for AD which emphasize obsessional and narrow patterns of interest; revises these criteria in 1991
1989	Peter Szatmari	Proposes diagnostic criteria for AD which emphasize social isolation
1991	Hans Asperger	1944 paper is translated into English for the first time and published in Uta Frith's edited book, *Autism and Asperger Syndrome*
1993	ICD-10	Diagnostic category for PDDs expanded from two diagnoses (AuD, PDD-NOS) to five, adding Rett's, CDD, and for the first time in DSM, Asperger's Disorder (AD)
1994	DSM IV	Follows ICD-10 in expanding PDD category to five diagnoses, including AuD, AD, and PDD-NOS

During these times, there were few organized systems of diagnostic classification for children (Rie 1971). The earliest systems did not differentiate schizophrenia or psychosis from autism and severe disorders of childhood were limited to infantile psychosis or childhood schizophrenia (Santangelo and Tsatsanis 2005). Leo Kanner (1957) who wrote the first textbook in English on child psychiatry in 1937, considered autism an early form of childhood schizophrenia traceable to maternal influence (Alexander and Selesnick 1966) and his earliest writings reflect the thinking of his time. In this context therefore, it is no surprise that he borrows the term "autism" from Bleuler. As research and theories expanded the understanding of the role of mother-child relationships (Bender 1952; Bowlby 1952; Klein 1954; Mahler 1968) and considered biological, physiological, and genetic factors as well as social, cultural, and emotional connections, Kanner shifted his views of autism toward an understanding of it as a genetic and organic disorder (Kanner 1957, 1958).

It was in this context that Kanner and Asperger were both observing and working with children, typically labeled with childhood schizophrenia. Understandably, these children's unusual, detached, withdrawn, unpredictable, often uncontrollable, behaviors, were hard to explain or categorize, based on what was known at the time. At the time, most theories maintained mental health or emotional causes to explain behavior and there were several proposed to explain the behavior of autistic children in the first half of the twentieth century. While there remains a place for understanding the existence of severe mental illness in children (i.e., childhood schizophrenia) where poor reality testing, delusions and hallucinations, inadequate ego functioning, and out of control behavior may dominate or significantly influence a child's existence, it is clear now that this is only one part of a broader picture of childhood diagnosis with the coinciding presence of a very separate and distinct category of children with ASD alongside other severe mental disorders. It is now imperative that the treating clinician be aware of the existence and range and the type of disorders possible, but also be aware of the need and importance of making clear and specific distinctions between these disorders.

Later developments – Kanner and autism

Leo Kanner and Hans Asperger were both born in Austria at the turn of the twentieth century and were trained in Vienna, although it is believed that they never met each other. Kanner, who was ten years older than Asperger, emigrated to the United States in 1924 and began on a geographically separate, but conceptually similar path to Asperger. It was while working at Johns Hopkins Hospital in Baltimore that he reported detailed descriptions of children he was observing and working with who presented with problems and disturbance from birth which resulted in a particular and clearly observable constellation of later problems different from those of childhood schizophrenia. His seminal 1943 paper, entitled, "Autistic Disturbances of Affective Contact" (Kanner 1973), described a childhood disturbance not previously understood or acknowledged. Kanner's description of 11 children focused on the core issues he described as autistic aloneness, an insistence on sameness, and islets of ability, and he introduced the label Early Infantile Autism, to describe these children.

The autistic aloneness that Kanner described included what appeared to be a total shutdown from outside stimulation characteristic of these children, apparently replaced by versions of their own internal world, presumably safer and better fitted to the child's needs and less psychologically demanding. The insistence on sameness that Kanner described was reflected in the repetitive and stereotypic movements, behaviors, verbalizations, and preoccupations that often dominated these children's interactions with the world. Kanner's reference to islets of ability provided descriptions of children with a range of abilities that included many with profound cognitive deficiencies to those with average or higher intelligence, advanced vocabulary, and excellent memory, which could occur in one or several areas of cognitive functioning.

Kanner's research became the basis for an understanding of what came to be known and described as Early Infantile Autism or Childhood Autism and which separated this category diagnostically from Childhood Schizophrenia. Following Kanner's description (simultaneously reported by Asperger in Vienna, but unknown to others outide of Germany), other views began to emerge and to consider broader, non-emotional considerations and causes, including the view that organicity and genetics may play a dominant role in the development of Kanner's autism.

Overall, Kanner's work formed the basis for our understanding of autism and the subsequent use of the term, "autism," in its modern sense. He provided a structure from which further research and understanding could begin to delineate differences within this autistic range of functioning, such as differences in autistic children's needs for internal and external stimulation and how these differ from normal children. His description of children with early infantile autism emphasized the social detachment and withdrawal of these children from the world around them and triggered interest in understanding the reasons about how and why this occurs. His use of the term autism emphasized the self-absorption and withdrawal he observed, yet disagreed with the view of many at the time that these children were demonstrating a psychotic or schizophrenic reaction or disorder or that they were reacting primarily as a result of emotional, familial, or environmental factors.

Following Kanner's 1943 paper which stimulated broader thinking and views of childhood diagnoses, shifts toward more developmental and neurological approaches gained momentum. It was Kanner's work at this time that provided the impetus to more clearly separate and differentiate mental disorders of childhood, such as childhood schizophrenia, from disorders considered to have a primary organic basis such as early infantile autism. From this, an increased desire to understand the role of organic, biological, and genetic factors in children gained impetus. Nevertheless, confusion continued regarding the differentiation between schizophrenia and autism, with some believing "that autism was the earliest manifestation of schizophrenia" (Bernet and Dulcan 2007) or a distinct type of childhood psychosis (Lovaas, Young, and Newsom 1978).

Kanner's 1943 article, "Autistic Disturbance of Affective Contact," published in the now defunct journal *Nervous Child*, defined early childhood autism as consisting of:

1. "an extreme autistic aloneness that, wherever possible disregards, ignores, shuts out anything that comes to the child from outside and includes a profound lack of affective contact with other people"

2. "anxiously obsessive desire for the preservation of sameness"

3. "a fascination for objects," but used only for repetitive activities

4. unusual, repetitive, pedantic language "not intended to serve interpersonal communication"

5. "islets (islands) of ability" (e.g., special skills, such as pensiveness, memory, motor skills, music, math, etc.).

Kanner's original diagnostic criteria for autism were modified in 1956 (Kanner and Eisenberg), noting several additional features apparent in many but not all of these children, which he considered important to the diagnosis, but not of primary importance. These additional features included:

6. impairment in nonverbal and social communication

7. a lack of coordinated motor movements (gross and/or fine motor) and a sense of clumsiness

8. repetitive, stereotypic movements

9. a range of unusual sensory experiences and needs

10. mimicking of others in nondeliberate and nonmalicious ways

11. poor behavioral regulation, often in response to disruption of routine or fixed patterns or to unusual arousal levels.

In discussing the eleven children he included in his article, Kanner described these children as having, "come into the world with innate inability to form the usual biologically provided affective contact with people" (Kanner 1973, first published 1943).

Later developments – Asperger and Asperger's Syndrome

At essentially the same time, Hans Asperger, a pediatrician, was working with similar types of children as Kanner at the children's clinic of the University of Vienna. In 1944, he published a paper describing four boys, taken from a representative sample of 200 children he had worked with, who were unable to effectively interact socially, exhibited repetitive and stereotypic behavior, but were capable of astounding achievements outside of their social inadequacies. He (as Kanner had done) used the term "autistic" to describe these boy's inabilities to connect and relate to the social world around them.

Asperger's paper, entitled, "Autistic Psychopathies of Childhood," was published in German in 1944, but was known to few outside the German speaking world until Lorna Wing referred to it in her research on autism in the late 1970s. It was subsequently translated and published in English (Asperger 1991) in Uta Frith's book on Asperger's Syndrome (Frith 1991). Asperger described "autistic psychopathy" as consisting of:

1. a "disturbance in social integration"
2. pedantic, peculiar language and the absence of reciprocity
3. impaired nonverbal and social communication
4. repetitive, stereotypic patterns of activities and play
5. isolated areas of special skills and interests.

Asperger also made mention of several additional areas of concern including;

6. good vocabulary and excellent logical thinking
7. unusual sensory responses and experiences
8. poorly coordinated movements and clumsiness
9. poor behavioral self-regulation.

Asperger described these children he studied as having, "a common fundamental disturbance...of contact" with other individuals who they came in contact with (Asperger 1991; 1979). Asperger's descriptions are amazingly similar to those of Kanner although it appears that Asperger's group appeared somewhat higher functioning in many cognitive areas.

Both Kanner and Asperger observed children who did not appear to fit the diagnostic classifications available at the time (i.e., infantile psychosis, childhood schizophrenia), but who exhibited qualities of autistic aloneness, preoccupations, and insistence on sameness (Kanner 1973). Kanner's use of the term infantile autism and Asperger's autistic psychopathy were initial attempts to differentiate and redefine these groups.

Kanner and Asperger separately were both clearly struggling to understand the autistic qualities they were observing when represented in different groups of children. The diagnoses of infantile psychosis and childhood schizophrenia focused on the emotional detachment and social withdrawal, but these diagnoses appeared inadequate for the subgroup of children Kanner described in his 1943 paper and Asperger in his 1944 paper.

Kanner's work, at the forefront of autism research, became widely known and recognized, rapidly becoming an integral part of childhood diagnosis. Asperger's work on the other hand, was published in German at the end of the Second World War, was not widely disseminated, and remained essentially unknown to most in the field until the 1980s. Nevertheless, Asperger's paper is strikingly similar to Kanner's in many ways. They both described children who were unable to integrate themselves socially or to form appropriate social relationships with others and who demonstrated unusual repetitive and stereotypic patterns of language, behavior, and movement. Kanner's reference to islets of ability appears more narrow than Asperger's description of "particular originality of thought and experience, which may well lead to exceptional achievements in later life" (Asperger 1991). It is likely that Asperger was working with a higher functioning group of autistic children, those later referred to diagnostically with HFA and AD. Both however, saw these groups as quite separate and distinct from children characterized as schizophrenic or with primarily emotional disorders.

> Both [Kanner and Asperger] recognized as prominent features in autism the poverty of social interaction and the failure of communication; highlighted stereotypic behavior, isolated special interests, outstanding skills and resistance to change; insisted on a clear separation from child-hood schizophrenia … On all the major features of autism Kanner and Asperger are in agreement. (Frith 1991, p.10)

Further developments

Kanner's research triggered the examination and exploration of autistic children and the establishment of separate criteria for autism as distinct from other disorders of childhood in ways that would define this area for the next half-century. However, confusion continued for decades around terminology and diagnostic classification and for a significant period of time, infantile psychosis and infantile autism continued to be used interchangeably. Nevertheless, Kanner's research continued to create separation between these groups and was gradually fortified by the ongoing work of other researchers throughout the world, including Uta Frith, Christopher Gillberg, Ivar Lovaas, Michael Rutter, Eric Shopler, Peter Szatmari, Lorna Wing, and others. Following this renewed interest in ASD in the late 1970s and 1980s, multiple sets of criteria for ASD were published (Frith 1991; Gillberg 1983; Szatmari, Brenner, and Nagy 1989; Wing 1981), including Kanner's (Kanner and Eisenberg 1956) and Asperger's (1979) own modifications.

However, despite the progress demonstrated in understanding these children, psychiatric and psychological research by others continued directed toward a constitutional, familial, and emotional explanation for these autistic behaviors in children, resulting in theories of inadequate bonding, poor parenting, and innate inabilities of the child to adapt. While there were many children fitting these descriptions, these explanations were subsequently viewed and proven inaccurate when applied to the subgroup of autistic individuals.

By the 1960s, autism was being viewed primarily as a completely separate syndrome from other childhood mental disorders, likely with genetic rather than emotional origins, demonstrated by significant impairments in several areas, including language and communication, social interaction, imagination, reality responses, and motor movements. As frequently occurs, many major researchers in the field, particularly at the higher end of the spectrum (e.g., HFA, AD), developed or employed their own unique set of diagnostic criteria, and while there was some sharing and overlap of many characteristics, there was no overall uniformity. This resulted in much confusion about which criteria were the best, the most useful, the most clinically appropriate, most research appropriate, most empirically based, etc.

Asperger's work, remaining essentially unknown, had little opportunity to impact this process in any way, until it was unearthed and rediscovered in 1981, and subsequently applied to the growing interest and understanding of autism and related disorders at that time, primarily by Lorna Wing, working in Great Britain. In her research, Wing was observing many children who did not fit current descriptions of the autistic child, but who still appeared to fit within the broadest definitions of autism, resulting in her use of the term "autistic continuum" which later she adjusted to "autistic spectrum." This allowed for a wide range of descriptions and symptoms related to autism to be included, based on where on the continuum the individual was considered to exist, using nine different criteria each ranging from profound to mild (Wing 1991). Thus at the lower end of the spectrum were the severely autistic individuals with profound disabilities, no or quite poor language or communication, very limited capacity to interact or engage others, repetitive, ritualistic or stereotypic behaviors and verbalizations, and the absence of imaginative, flexible, symbolic play and thinking. At the other, higher end of the spectrum, were those considered as high functioning autistic individuals HFA, with average to superior intelligence, appropriate and often advanced language development, but with peculiar, pedantic, and odd usage of language, very limited to quite variable capacity to interact or engage others in appropriate social interactions, and generally some form of repetitive, stereotypic, or ritualized behavior or area of interest.

However, even at the higher ends of the autism spectrum, this group of HFA individuals did not appear homogeneous within themselves and significant variation and differences were still observed. While this group demonstrated no cognitive delays, language and communication were quite variable, with some individuals having no delays and others with quite deficient functioning, as was the ability to learn and use social interactional skills. Studies that followed appeared to indicate the possibility of a separate syndrome from traditional autism and from HFA and which was characterized primarily by social deficits, maladaptive behaviors (stereotypic, repetitive, ritualistic), and problems with pragmatic communication, but without significant cognitive or language delays.

During this time, Wing described 34 cases of children and adults with autism whose profiles of abilities appeared to have great resemblance to those described in the little known and little referenced report by Hans Asperger (1991). Wing subsequently used the term Asperger's Syndrome to describe the new diagnostic category which she placed within the autistic continuum (Wing 1981). Research and observation continued through the 1980s to refine and differentiate autism and autism-like disorders.

Following Wing's (1981) description of Asperger's work as it related to similarities she reported in her own studies, her use of the label Asperger's Syndrome, and translation of his original article (Asperger 1991), interest in "autistic psychopathy" as distinct from autism was raised. Asperger's Syndrome was used to identify this high functioning group of ASD individuals who demonstrated the "triad of social impairments" Wing had observed, impairments in social relationships, communication, and make-believe play, differentiating this group from the traditional autistic and HFA groups, but acknowledging that AD was still likely one of several categories within the "autistic continuum" (Wing 1988). Interest in autism research and what came to be known as "autism spectrum disorders" moved rapidly forward through the latter part of the twentieth century, focusing primarily on diagnostic issues, causal factors, subtypes and classification, and treatment and intervention models. As mentioned, works by Michael Rutter, Eric Schopler, Leo Kanner, Uta

Frith, Christopher Gillberg, Fred Volkmer, and Lorna Wing were particularly influential during this time.

Diagnostic categories

Definitions of infantile autism were officially recognized and adopted by the World Health Organization in 1978 in their *International Classification of Disease 9th Edition* (ICD-9) manual (World Health Organization 1978) and by the American Psychiatric Association in the Diagnostic and Statistical Manual of Mental Health Disorders – Third Edition (DSM III) (American Psychiatric Association 1980) with later modifications in DSM III-R (American Psychiatric Association 1987). At that point in time, DSM III and DSM III-R (and ICD-9 as well) contained a main category of Pervasive Developmental Disorders (PDD) which consisted of two subcategories of Infantile Autism (the term used in DSM III)/Autistic Disorder (AuD) (the modified term used in DSM III-R) and Pervasive Developmental Disorder – Not Otherwise Specified (PDD-NOS). Individuals who met criteria for autism were given the diagnosis of AuD and any individuals who did not meet full criteria for AuD but were still considered to have a PDD were given the diagnosis of PDD-NOS, in what became a large residual category (e.g., atypical autism).

In 1988, the first international conference on Asperger's Syndrome was held in London, attended by most of the key figures in the autism/Asperger's field at the time. No consensus on diagnostic criteria was reached (Szatmari 1991) and several authors and researchers proposed their own diagnostic criteria applying to ASD. Gillberg and Gillberg (1989) published a set of diagnostic criteria on AD, subsequently revised in 1991 (Gillberg 1991), as did Szatmari and colleagues (Szatmari *et al.* 1989), and Wing (1991).

Subsequently, ICD-10 was published in 1993 and DSM IV in 1994. Both adopted a broader categorization of PDD, continuing to highlight AuD's central place, but now with four additional diagnostic categories, Rett's Disorder, Childhood Disintegrative Disorder (CDD), AD, and PDD-NOS. The publication of ICD-10 and DSM IV also marked the initial inclusion of AD in a published diagnostic manual. Also within the PDD, Rett's Disorder and CDD were given separate diagnostic classifications and were no longer included within the broad residual diagnosis of PDD-NOS.

Within DSM IV, PDD are considered a broad and diverse group of diagnostic categories with AuD, AD, and PDD-NOS considered and referred to as ASD. ASD reflect a broad, often ambiguous continuum or spectrum of autistic disorders. Although clustered alongside ASD in DSM IV under PDD, Rett's Disorder and CDD appear to reflect qualitatively different types of developmental disorders with likely different medical, genetic, neurological, cognitive, and biological underpinnings, and as such, these are not considered ASD (see Figure 2.1).

Within the DSM IV category of PDD, AuD is a pervasive developmental disorder characterized by significant impairments in language and communication (usually both semantic and pragmatic), together with repetitive, restrictive, stereotypic thoughts, actions, or behaviors, and with significant social impairments. Intellectual functioning is below normal in approximately 75 percent of autistic individuals with the remaining 25 percent with average or better intellectual functioning often referred to as HFA.

Asperger's Disorder, added to DSM IV and ICD-10 only in the latest editions, is defined as a pervasive developmental disorder characterized by significant impairment in social interaction which may also occur together with repetitive, restrictive, or stereotypic thoughts, actions, or behaviors. Typically in AD, there are no significant functional (semantic) language or communication impairments, although pragmatic language difficulties are common, and intellectual functioning is usually average or better.

For those individuals who do not fit criteria for AuD or AD or another PDD, but who still exhibit significant impairments in one or more of the key areas (social interaction; repetitive, restrictive, or stereotypic thoughts, actions, or behaviors; language or communication), then the category of PDD-NOS may be applied. However, this has resulted in a fairly broad, residual, and default category for individuals exhibiting some combinations of PDD/autistic-like behaviors.

Despite the modifications and inclusion of additional PDD in DSM IV and ICD-10, confusion and disagreement have continued around diagnostic categorization and diagnostic criteria, particularly focused on AD and the differentiation between AuD (especially HFA) and AD. Despite its inclusion in DSM IV as a PDD distinct from AuD and PDD-NOS, the criteria used do not help to classify or differentiate it from higher functioning forms of autism (e.g., HFA). Many clinicians have continued to conceptualize AD as a mild variant of autism (Ghaziuddin, Leininger, and Tsai 1995) and to continue to view AD as a spectrum disorder rather than to view it from a categorical perspective (Attwood 2007; Leekham *et al.* 2000) as found in DSM IV.

Other professionals have established and maintained their own descriptions and criteria for autism and ASD separate from DSM IV and ICD-10 and this remains a central problem in establishing the boundaries of who is and who is not considered within the specific diagnoses. More recent attempts to further differentiate AD from other autistic disorders have spurred further research into all aspects of ASD and PDDs, but with continuing controversy and disagreement. This occurs in nomenclature. What are the boundaries of: PDD, AuD, ASD, HFA, and AD? This occurs in diagnosis. Which criteria is most accurate, most applicable, or most valid: DSM IV (its predecessors or soon to be released DSM V), ICD-10, specific criteria delineated by Wing (1981), Gillberg and Gillberg (1989), Szatmari and colleagues (1989), or others? Finally, disagreement and controversy occurs even to the extent of questioning whether AD does in fact exist as a separate diagnostic entity, is a subtype of another disorder (e.g., of autism as an ASD), or is solely the result of symptom overlap with other disorders and therefore takes on the "look" of a well-differentiated disorder or diagnostic category.

Thus, Asperger's Syndrome or Disorder, a term preferred to Asperger's original label, autistic psychopathy, has become associated with a form of autism thought to include the key autism features of: impairments in social interaction and restricted repetitive, and stereotyped, patterns of behavior, interests, and activities, but to not include impairments in communication (i.e., language delays) or cognition (i.e., retardation).

Questions regarding diagnostic categorization and nomenclature and diagnostic distinctions have yet to be answered satisfactorily and further research and study must continue and will be necessary to clarify these issues. There is no attempt here to decide these issues, but only to add to the informational base available for future decisions to be made.

Chapter 4

Additional and Alternative Definitions for ASD

In the years since Kanner's and Asperger's descriptions of autistic children, several prominent authors and researchers on Autism Spectrum Disorders (ASD) have developed and used specific, but somewhat different, diagnostic criteria in their research and writings. Although there is significant overlap and some consistency from one set of criteria to another, there is also significant variation and disagreement. As such, the measurement of ASD and subsequent research is at times dependent on the definitions used and at least five different definitions have been employed in ASD research alone (Volkmar *et al.* 2004). Each researcher in their own way has struggled with the issue of diagnostic differentiation between Autistic Disorder (AuD), High Functioning Autism (HFA), Asperger's Disorder (AD), other Pervasive Developmental Disorder (PDD) (i.e., Pervasive Developmental Disorder – Not Otherwise Specified, PDD-NOS), and of course, the possibilities of other intervening diagnoses or "pseudo-diagnoses."

This ongoing diagnostic debate along the autism spectrum is more prominent at the higher end of the continuum and has to do with the differentiation (or lack of it) between AuD, HFA, and AD. Since the group interventions described here are most useful with ASD children who function toward the higher end of the autism spectrum, particularly as it relates to communication and cognitive functioning, some of the varied and alternative definitions for AD are provided here.

Wing's (1981) description of individuals along the autism spectrum are the most detailed. As a result of her own research and review of the available autism and AD literature, she initially provided a triad of behavioral symptom manifestations necessary for an ASD diagnosis, requiring:

1.	impaired social relationships
2.	impaired communication
3.	impaired make-believe play.

These criteria were later modified (Wing 1991) to include:

1.	impairment in social reciprocity
2.	unusual, odd, pedantic, and stereotypic speech
3.	poor nonverbal and facial communication
4.	insistence on repetition and sameness
5.	specific, often highly narrow, interests
6.	poor motor coordination.

And modified further with the addition of impairments in:

7.	social imagination
8.	sensory inputs
9.	repetitive, stereotypic movements.

In addressing broader ASD issues, Wing expanded her list to include criteria typically seen in varying degrees in individuals falling on the autistic continuum. Each criteria exists within a range from profound impairment to no impairment. While she places primary emphasis on the triad of social impairments, she asserts the importance of understanding other variables, including their severity, in understanding these individuals and in making proper and appropriate diagnosis.

At the same time, following years of research in Sweden, Christopher Gillberg (Gillberg and Gillberg 1989) developed a similar set of criteria for AD, but did not include impairments in sensory inputs or social imagination. He focused his criteria on elaborating and further defining the primary core deficit areas of social interaction, narrow interests, routinized behavior, verbal and nonverbal communications, and motor issues. Meanwhile in Canada, Peter Szatmari and colleagues (Szatmari, Bremner and Nagy 1989) were constructing their own set, emphasizing social impairments as the primary key deficits, along with communication (verbal and nonverbal).

Nevertheless, DSM and ICD, despite their limitations and criticisms (Attwood 2007), continued to be the most widely used criteria in research and clinical diagnosis. The ICD-10 revision in 1993 and the DSM IV revision in 1994 were nearly identical. Both included AD for the first time, with its own separate diagnosis within PDD. The AD criteria in each however, include only two key categories, social impairment and repetitive, stereotypic behavior, excluding language or communication impairment and cognitive delays or impairments, both of which were included only under AuD.

Both ICD-10 and DSM-IV diagnostic criteria for AD include: 1. significant impairments in reciprocal social interaction, defined by difficulties with nonverbal behaviors such as eye-to-eye gaze, facial expression, body postures, and gestures to regulate social interaction, difficulties with developmentally appropriate peer relationships, an inability to spontaneously seek or share enjoyment, interests, or achievements with other people, and problems with social or emotional reciprocity; 2. restricted, repetitive and stereotyped patterns of behavior, interests, and activities, defined by an intense and overwhelming focus or preoccupation with one or more stereotyped and restricted patterns of interest, an inflexible adherence to routines or rituals, stereotyped and repetitive motor mannerisms, and persistent focus or preoccupations with parts of objects. These must cause clinically significant impairment in social, occupational, or other important areas of functioning. In AD however, there are no indications of functional language impairment (e.g., mechanics), although pragmatic language may be deficient, and there are no indications of significantly impaired intelligence or cognition.

In summary, definitions for ASD include a varying combination of criteria, but always address impairments in social interaction, communication (verbal and nonverbal), and behavioral issues (e.g., restricted, repetitive, stereotypic behavior; rigid adherence to routines; restrictive, narrow interests). Impairments in motor issues, sensory inputs, or imaginative/pretend play are included in some, but not all criteria sets.

Chapter 5

Social Development and Children with ASD

Overview

The socialization process includes two interrelated concepts of development: 1. social competence, the capacities and abilities to recognize, understand, and engage in appropriate reciprocal interchange with one or more individuals; and 2. social skills, the actual tools or learned skills for appropriate social interactions and social communication.

Social competence relies on innate capacities and acquired abilities and relates to the underlying structures and processes present in the individual and necessary for subsequent development. Social competence provides the foundation on which further development can proceed, and is the focus, attention, interest, understanding, and need to engage in social interchange with other human beings.

Social skills are the mechanisms through which individuals make contact, initiate, engage, and follow through in reciprocal social interchange. They are actual tools or skills needed for the socialization process to move forward and for meaningful relationships to be attempted and to succeed. For human beings, social competence provides the capacity to learn socialization skills, that is, the "legs" on which individuals can move forward, while social skills are the tool and techniques, the actual process of "learning to walk."

Early development

Most children with Autism Spectrum Disorders (ASD) suffer from some degree of impairment in social interaction. This may involve impairment in social competence, the underlying processes necessary for further development, in social skills, the tools necessary for the social interchange to actually occur, or the combined effects of the impairments in both social competence and social skill development. Because children with ASD will differ, often dramatically, from one child to the next in the degree and extent of their social impairments, there is no "typical child with ASD." In terms of social impairments, children with higher levels of severity and lower levels of functioning will be more noticeable at an early age, often during the first year of life. This may include the child's inability or unwillingness to make appropriate eye contact, to respond to a parent's smile or facial expressions, to track interesting objects or loud sounds in their environment, to seek physical contact or cuddling, or to initiate interactions with the world outside of themselves. They may appear distant, disinterested, or disengaged in the social contacts that most other children thrive on.

However, it is not uncommon for children who are higher functioning on the autism spectrum (i.e., High Functioning Autism (HFA), Asperger's Disorder (AD), some Pervasive Developmental Disorder – Not Otherwise Specified (PDD-NOS)), to appear quite typical in their interactions during infancy and early childhood. This may relate to the low severity, low frequency, or reduced need for expression of the behavior. It may appear as if the child is choosing not to respond (i.e., has the ability, but "chooses" not to implement), is not sufficiently motivated to respond (i.e., another sibling readily initiates for the child), has few opportunities to respond (i.e., limited number of individuals involved in their day to day activities), or the child's responses may be considered within the range of normal functioning for that age (i.e., "he will play with Lego all day if you let him").

With children with AD, language development may occur early and is often advanced, making these children appear more "mature" at young ages, when in fact, social competencies and/or social skills may be quite limited, overshadowed by their competencies in language areas. By preschool, unusual or deficient social interactions are typically noticed in broader, peer-based environments and brought to the parents' attention. This may include a range of possible behaviors, including stilted, pedantic, idiosyncratic language, solitary play, a lack of understanding or empathy for others, or an inability to make or maintain friendships.

With the highest functioning ASD children, it is not unusual for social problems to go undetected until entering elementary school settings. Given the range of differences between ASD children, they may be considered only as quirky, a bit odd or unusual, as loners, or just as socially inept. In fact, the average age of diagnosis of AD is reported between eight and ten years old (Attwood 2007).

Typical social concerns reported by parents/caretakers during the early stages of the social developmental process and by school personnel of children ultimately diagnosed with ASD often include:

1. lack of attachment and "bonding"

2. poor eye contact or an eye gaze that fails to follow the parent/caretaker

3. does not greet or respond to the parent/caretaker spontaneously

4. does not seek out parent or others for comfort

5. little or no expression of emotion or inappropriate expression of emotion

6. does not understand "personal space."

Later in development, other behaviors reported by parents/caretakers and school personnel of children ultimately diagnosed with ASD include:

7. failure to attend or to "connect" in social relationships

8. aloofness from or disinterest in social relationships

9. lack of empathy or concern for others feelings or emotions

10. lack of social reciprocity

11. lack of social imagination

12. does not prefer team sports or activities.

In addition, parents of ASD children generally report a range of behaviors quite different from those normally reported by parents/caretakers of typically developing children including:

13. does not seek out parent/caretaker to engage in play

14. bedtime routines become highly ritualized and lack comfort and nurturance

15. gets "stuck" on tasks or activities and cannot let go

16. blurts out whatever he or she may be thinking

17. is frequently taken advantage of, teased, bullied, or victimized.

While there is growing research in many of the areas that contribute to successful social interaction (e.g., facial recognition, joint attention, empathy, theory of mind, imagination, etc.), there is no clear understanding why these impairments in social interactions occur in ASD children. Nevertheless, they clearly present significant barriers for the ASD child in managing and coping with the social world they must exist within. Helping children with ASD to understand their own profile of strengths and limitations, to understand the world around them, and to manage social interaction and social interchange effectively, are the primary goals of the interventions described in this book. In this context, social development from the perspective of normal development and from the perspective of the individual with ASD is described.

Social cognition

Normal social development follows a generally consistent and systematic path beginning at birth. Much attention, particularly over the past fifty years, has been paid to the origins and developmental pathways of social competence. There is strong emerging data supporting the view that newborn infants demonstrate significant capacities for the perception, initiation, and direction of early physical and social interactions and from birth are processing and responsive to significant amounts of sensory (visual, auditory, etc.) information.

Newborn infants are capable of facial expressions, imitations, and behaviors, which initiate, encourage, and reinforce, social interactions with their surroundings. It is well known that infants are most responsive to their own mother's and primary caretaker's actions and reactions, particularly when these involve facial expressions and positive interactions (e.g., smiling, singing, marked inflections, etc.). However, infants also react, but in different ways, to less well known and stranger interactions and negative interactions (e.g., a scowl, frown, yelling, etc.).

Attachment research (e.g., Bowlby 1952) is quite explicit about the importance of the bond between the child and caretaker and its role in social emotional development. Evident within the first year of life, attachment and bonding allows the child to perform an ever increasing series of necessary developmental tasks (e.g., exploration, sharing, fantasy), influenced by parental, familial, and environmental reactions and responses. In this way, many of the child's innate social abilities and social-emotional response patterns are shaped by these interactions of the child's personality-temperament with caretakers, family members, peers, and other environmental influences. Through eye contact, facial expressions, sounds, and body movements, the infant provides signals to its environment which trigger social interaction. These signals are followed by responses from the environment, such as food/sustenance, physical contact, warmth, cuddling, and other forms of comfort and physical and social stimulation.

It is this process of normal social development which results in increasing social and reciprocal interactions that meet the needs of both the child and his caretakers that appears to be absent or derailed for the ASD individual. In contrast to the normal child, the ASD child may lack the capacity to establish and sustain eye contact, may not be capable of using facial expressions to convey feelings and emotions, may not be able to create verbalizations that appropriately match or fit with the social situation, and may not accurately interpret or understand the nature and meaning of interactional cues given to them by others. Many of these factors, such as the absence of eye contact/eye gaze, facial misperception (Klin *et al.* 2002), inattention, inappropriate verbalizations, misinterpretation of verbal and nonverbal cuing, and other social interactional breakdowns (Barry *et al.* 2003; Klin *et al.* 2002), have been reported as core deficits in ASD contributing directly to the social impairments seen in ASD individuals.

It is clear from birth, social development assumes a two-way reciprocal interaction, that is, how each individual in the interaction responds to the other determines the depth and quality of the interchange. While the ASD child may be capable of perceiving and processing the requests for socially appropriate interchanges (e.g., "mother is smiling at me"), they may lack the capacity to spontaneously respond in kind (e.g., look when their name is called, smile when someone smiles at them) (Dawson *et al.* 1998), or be delayed in their responding (possibly a cognitive processing problem), thus altering the social interchange (i.e., the other individual does not receive the expected and socially appropriate response), derailing the reciprocal process. When this aspect of social development (i.e., social reciprocity) is derailed from an early age, then the individual's ability to learn and benefit from all the social interactions and interchanges which will subsequently occur will be severely limited.

In the non-ASD population, social development research (e.g., Clarke-Stewart and Koch 1983) clearly indicate infants inability to thrive and survive adequately when human interaction is not provided, is significantly inadequate, or is poorly matched to the infants needs. Therefore, it is not difficult to understand the views and beliefs of the early to mid twentieth century that children who did not possess or could not develop appropriate and adequate social competence and social interactive skills were the result of a failure or inadequacy in parenting/caretaking skills and abilities when viewed through the lens that all children are born with certain innate capacities for social interactive and social reciprocal interchange. It was the emergence of the view that the child him/herself may have been born without those necessary innate social capacities (e.g., Asperger 1991; Kanner 1973) that resulted in consideration of a broader range of possibilities to account for the child's social impairments.

As children grow and these social exchanges and social interactions increase, evolve developmentally, and are reinforced, they are increasingly employed and more selectively used as they are fine tuned to fit the individual's needs and their environment. Providing a foundation on which subsequent language and cognitive development can grow, social interaction takes its prominent place as a necessary and critical piece of developmental growth and maturity.

It appears that ASD children may follow a different developmental path than typical non-ASD children (Barry *et al.* 2003), although current research is not yet clear on this issue, partly due to the significant variability from individual child to child with ASD and the ongoing controversy over diagnostic differentiation and categorization. This path for many ASD children begins with what appears to be normal social development, usually the first year or two of life, then abruptly stalls, usually within the second or third year of life. However, for others development may appear derailed from birth.

The developmental path for both the typical and the ASD child, however, is dependent upon the innate capacities for socialization that the child is born with (i.e., the underlying structures or processes), enabling development to move forward through a consistent and relatively predictable series of stages which include the acquisition of social skills appropriate to the child's age and stage. If the innate developmental capacities of a child are derailed, either prior to birth, at birth, or in the first years of life, then the developmental path is dependent upon the capacities the child does possess to facilitate moving forward and progressing through appropriate developmental stages as they are confronted. It appears that these innate capacities are not fixed or consistent in the ASD population and wide variation between groups and individuals occurs.

Nevertheless, for both the typical child with adequate innate developmental capacities and the child with derailed or deficient aspects of social development, subsequent social competence will depend on the child's abilities (or inabilities) to learn and develop the necessary social skills and tools for effective social interaction and social communication. Clearly, for the ASD child, who may possess limited innate developmental capacities, the socialization and social learning process will be extremely difficult.

Stages of the socialization process

Normal socialization in most individuals follows a predictable pattern of development that includes a fixed set of stages beginning at birth. Each stage consists of a series or cluster of learning experiences and interactions with objects, individuals, and groups, providing a foundation for subsequent experiences and interactions to take place. While the experiences and interactions within each stage are qualitatively different from one stage to the next, they are reliant on the development that occurs in previous stages. Thus, both development and progress or deficits and derailment at one stage will affect all subsequent experiences and interactions occurring at later stages. Understanding the socialization process, its developmental flow, and its movement through stages, provides a basis for understanding and treating issues that arise with children with ASD within a group-based setting.

Stage 1

In the first days and months following birth, infants respond and react to both internal and external stimuli in their environment with the sole purpose of getting their basic needs met. As they grow and develop and as their basic needs are met in a consistent and predictable manner, they respond more actively to an ever growing range of sensory and social stimuli. They learn to attend to and progressively differentiate sounds, faces, and types of interactions (e.g., friendly vs. hostile). The beginnings of basic trust in others, particularly caretakers who respond to their needs, develop during this stage.

Stage 2

By the second half of the first year of life, infants have begun a sophisticated process of imitation of sounds, simple acts, and gestures, as a form of engaging and connecting with others. This process takes on an increasingly more active function as the child is no longer responding passively to another's initiations, but actively soliciting the attention and involvement of others through their own actions and behavior. The beginnings of solitary play as a means of learning about the world can also be seen emerging as another way of learning about and exploring one's environment. The beginnings of an individuation process take hold and solidify during this stage.

Stage 3

By the second year of life, toddlers now become mobile *and* active in seeking out increasing amounts of external stimulation and social contact. They begin to actively respond and adapt to other's needs and to cooperate in joint tasks and activities. Solitary play no longer appears completely satisfactory as engaging others in parallel play begins to take precedence and being with others and seeking their attention become paramount. During this stage, the child's sense of autonomy increases and differentiates from the control imposed solely by others.

Stage 4

By early childhood, social interactions increase at a dramatic rate as connections begin to extend beyond the family to self-initiated social contacts and interactions with others. Children begin to seek out groups of other children, particularly similar age peers, as a preferred social situation to solitary play and primitive friendships begin to develop and take root. Adults are seen in the role of authority, as providers, and as protectors, but also figures from whom the child seeks independence in the early stages of autonomy. Self-initiative, more complete autonomy and sense of self, and imagination, develop rapidly during this stage.

Stage 5

By later childhood, self-control, independence, autonomy, and social networks become the central forces of social interactions. Social acceptance particularly within groups is highly valued and sought after and becomes a necessity for further social maturity and development to take place. Recognizing and understanding one's strengths and weaknesses occurs in increasingly more realistic ways and influences development and interactions during this stage.

Stage 6

By adolescence, the capacity for true friendships, meaningful interactions, mutual reciprocal interchanges, social intimacy, and empathy has evolved. While there may emerge an increased interest in independence and solitude, there is also an increased interest in the development of a set of individual and group values and standards apart from parents and adult authority, at times, triggering a rejection of adult value systems. Developing a true sense of one's personal identity both as an individual and as part of groups emerges during this stage.

Stage 7

Entering adulthood brings a level of maturity and intimacy to relationships and the capacity for long-term meaningful connections with others. These are highly valued and cherished and seen as goals as they provide a springboard further into mature phases of adulthood (e.g., marriage, career, parenthood).

Social competence

In typical development, social competence consists of several different aspects including the ability to recognize a situation requiring social interaction, the ability to initiate a social interchange, the ability to understand its content and meaning and to move it forward, and the ability to respond to the range of stimuli available in the situation (i.e., engage in and follow a discussion or play activity). In essence, social competence is the capacity to engage in a reciprocal process of shared experience with another individual or individuals (Shores 1987). While extremely complex in nature, this process includes the capacity to move through stages of socialization while learning, refining, and mastering a broad range of social interactions and to attain and maintain developmentally appropriate levels of social recognition and awareness, social interest and motivation, social comprehension, memory, learning, social skill development, and social-emotional affective states (e.g., sympathy, empathy). Social competence provides the foundation and capacities to learn and make use of specific social skills.

In essence, the development of social competence is embedded within the progression through stages of socialization. It involves the presence of innate capacities for socialization, the developmental thrust pushing for increased social contact, adequate and sustaining parental, familial, caretaker, and environmental experiences matching stage-based social needs, and the capacities to learn and retain needed skills. In a group based approach, each of these issues must be considered and addressed as the group is constructed, as individual and group goals are formulated, and as tasks and activities are planned, and modified on a regular basis.

Social skills

Social skills are defined as complex sets of behaviors which allow an individual to engage in positive, mutually reciprocal and beneficial social interactions (Gumpel 1994). Possessing a range of social skills may allow the individual to initiate, maintain, manipulate, or solidify a social interaction, thereby creating a "social relationship." This may also have secondary gains of improving social status (Odom and McConnell 1985).

Social skills are the actual tools or signposts learned as one traverses the developmental path that make the process of social competence work. Social skills are the actual ways to initiate, to engage, to communicate, and to respond to others when involved in an interchange. In other words, social competence is awareness of the existence of a social situation or impending social interaction, together with the desire and the ability to engage in a reciprocal social interchange (the underlying structure necessary to recognize, acknowledge, and implement in a social situation) while social skills provide the actual ways in which we perform in this situation (e.g., make eye contact, say hello, ask a question, listen and formulate a response, arrange a subsequent meeting, say goodbye).

ASD individuals all appear quite unique with social capacities that extend across a broad range of social competence and social skill strengths and deficits. In general however, most ASD individuals suffer from some degree of significant social impairments which may include some combinations of significant social competency deficits and social skills deficiencies. While some ASD individuals lack many or all aspects of social competence and, thus, social skills will be unable to develop appropriately, some possess sufficient social competency for the acquisition of some limited skills, yet many struggle with a broad range and variety of social competence and social skill deficits. The approach described here attempts to systematically assess the ASD individual's social abilities and skills and to thoughtfully place them in a social situation, i.e., small group, peer-based, structure based, skill-focused, and adult-monitored, where the individual's needs can be addressed. While ASD individuals benefit from a variety of different types of interventions, we believe that the core deficit in social interaction can be best addressed by focusing on social competency and social skills development within a group setting with peers monitored by adults. This setting provides the environment for learning about and understanding reciprocal social interchange and learning the skills needed to engage others successfully while at the same time experiencing relationships, connections, and emotional experiences as part of a group.

Specific social competencies and social skills targeted will relate to the ASD individual's specific needs which are assessed and considered during initial assessment described in Chapter 12 and elaborated in the goal setting process described in Chapters 11 and 12.

Social competencies viewed as essential for appropriate social development and which appear necessary in order to build adequate social skills, include:

1. recognition and understanding of the need for social interchange and the inherent complexity of social interchange

2. acknowledgement of the need and importance of experiencing and understanding what it means to be part of a group

3. development and enhancement of the capacity to create and sustain meaningful interpersonal relationships with others, especially peers

4. effective employment of the range of self-based functions, such as self-awareness, self-management, self-regulation and self-control, and insight

5. management and control of the stress and tension involved in approaching and interacting with others in social situations

6. sufficient development and functioning of attentional capacities, particularly those required for appropriate social interaction, such as joint attention

7. the capacity to consider and tolerate thoughts, actions, behaviors, and emotions of others so as to remain open and flexible in interactions with others

8. the capacity to be open and flexible in our thinking, actions, behaviors, and emotions so as to allow others to join us in social interchange

9. the capacity to move smoothly from one thought, issue, topic, action, or emotion to another without difficulty (i.e., rigid adherence, undue stress or tension, distractibility, disturbance of emotions)

10. recognition of sensory experiences when they occur and understanding how they impact and influence social interactions

11. the capacity to understand and appreciate the thoughts, actions, behaviors, and emotions of others as they occur in a range of personal and interpersonal situations (also described as having Theory of Mind)

12. recognition and management of emotions that arise in social interactions and understanding how they impact the social relationship.

Focusing on the building and enhancement of social competence as the foundation for social skill development provides an approach for the explicit teaching of necessary social skills. With an emphasis on group-based approaches which emphasize the development of the underlying social competence abilities, methods which teach the necessary social skills must include aspects of the following:

1. the social skills to be taught must be defined and connected to the overall social competency

2. the social skill must be broken down into simple steps that can be easily learned, practiced, and repeated in different situations

3. each skill or set of skills must be directly connected to individual and group goals as constructed within the group

4. there must be adequate opportunity for modeling by peers to enhance learning and reinforcement

5. mastery and success of the social skill must be adequately understood, integrated with other behaviors and interactions, and reinforced

6. behaviors which inhibit social interaction must be targeted for reduction and extinction

7. multiple strategies to complete a social skill interaction must be developed and implemented

8. skill instruction is considered dynamic, ready to be changed or modified at any point, to meet the needs and goals of the group

9. individual and group goals which focus on specific social skill development are evaluated systematically and progress assessed

10. those social skills selected and taught must emphasize carryover and generalization to real-life situations outside the group.

With the development of appropriate social competencies, the list of social skills contained in Figure 5.1 is viewed as only a small sample of the range of skills that may be targeted as essential for appropriate social development.

Figure 5.1 Selected social skills to be addressed

Entering a group

- Introductions of self
- Initiating a conversation
- Maintaining a conversation (Conversational skills)
- Expressing interest in others
- Following directions

Initiating and expanding discussions using personal information and preferences

- Soliciting personal information from others
- Sharing personal information relevant to the topic or discussion
- Taking turns in conversation, in activities, tasks, or games
- Acknowledging points/information that others contribute
- Following changes in topic
- Offering an opinion or suggestion

Playing by the rules

Asking for help

Regulating the intensity and quality of one's interactions

- Voice tone/voice volume
- Facial expressions

Understanding and respecting body space

Cooperation

- Sharing (of things that matter to the individual)
- Compromise
- Being a good sport
- Apologizing

Giving and receiving compliments and encouragement

- Giving and receiving criticism

Recognizing and using emotions in interactions

- Expressing feelings
- Assertiveness
- Disagreeing

Friendship

- Discussing and understanding what is a friend
- Discussing and understanding what is a friendship

Managing conflict and confrontation

- Confronting teasing, putdowns, or bullying in a group

Recognizing and interpreting verbal, nonverbal, and conceptual cues

- Understanding and using verbal interchanges
- Reading verbal signals
- Reading nonverbal signals

Using humor

Perspective taking

- Sympathy and empathy

Discussing and resolving decision-making issues

Discussing and resolving problem-solving issues

Exiting a group

- Ending a conversation

Dealing with loss, terminations, and goodbyes

- Recognizing the loss associated with goodbyes
- Expressing the loss associated with goodbyes
- Recognizing the feelings and emotions associated with goodbyes
- Creating memories to preserve the relationships
- Celebrating the loss, termination, or goodbyes
- Saving the loss, termination, or goodbyes
- Saying goodbyes

PART II

TREATING CHILDREN WITH AUTISM SPECTRUM DISORDERS

Part II addresses how to understand and manage several key factors that emerge in group interventions with ASD individuals. In particular, the key variables of stress, tension, and anxiety, of attention, of flexibility, change, and transition, and of managing and regulating affective and emotional responses, are highlighted. While this is not assumed or intended to be an exhaustive list of possible variables that could be addressed, these variables in particular are considered of primary importance to address and manage if appropriate group and social interactions, social competencies, and social skills are to be acquired.

Each key variable, of stress, tension, anxiety, of attention, of flexibility, change, and transition, and of managing and regulating affective and emotional responses, is initially considered separately as it applies to ASD individuals through a cognitive-developmental perspective. Issues of management and treatment are then considered and how they apply to the group-focused, peer-based, cognitive-developmental stage model which will be described in later chapters.

Chapter 6

Stress and Anxiety

Overview

This chapter describes a model for understanding stress, tension, and anxiety as experienced by the individual with Autism Spectrum Disorder (ASD). This includes a description of the ASD individual's attempts to maintain equilibrium and to manage and fend off stress and tension and how this often results in a downward spiral through a stress-tension-anxiety continuum into overload and meltdown. A second pathway resulting from increased stress and tension, a shift into a mode of rigidity/inflexibility in managing stress, tension and change will be discussed in Chapter 8.

While stress and anxiety are normally occurring human experiences, the ability to manage and to cope with them effectively is a combination of genetic predisposition, individual temperament traits, learned coping strategies, situational variables and factors, and external supports. Often the source of the stress, or point of tension, will determine the individual's capacity to manage or to deal with it effectively and adaptively. For example, a teacher giving the week's homework assignments may be managed differently than a parent reminder to complete those same assignments in a timely manner. Also, the same situation may be managed quite differently by different individuals. For example, one individual may cope quite effectively with test anxiety, barely registering any change in heart rate, pulse, skin response, or core body temperature, while another individual may experience several somatic reactions or even a panic attack in the same situation.

In the social domain, individuals young and old are called upon to confront a variety of different types of social interactions on a daily basis, each creating different degrees and levels of stress and each requiring a range of coping and management strategies. Certain situations may be managed with relative ease (e.g., greetings each morning as one arrives at work or school), while others may provoke intense or chronic stress (e.g., responding to a teacher question in class, a call from the boss). Learning how to anticipate these situations and to prepare for them using both innate and learned coping strategies is an important part of human development.

For the ASD individual, deficits and impairments in social competency and social skill development will affect and limit an individual's capacity to experience social interactions in normal ways, to understand their meaning, and to learn how to adapt and manage them effectively as one moves through each stage of social development. From an early age, the ASD individual may fail to make appropriate eye contact, fail to accurately read facial expressions, fail to understand subtle comments, or become confused and upset by another's negative reaction to something they say or do. Each of these experiences may produce some level of stress or tension.

Stress – what is it?

Stress is considered to be a state of disequilibrium (i.e., the stress response), triggered in an individual by a broad range of internally or externally generated stimuli (i.e., the stressor), which create a state of heightened arousal in the individual (Selye 1993). Coping is the capacity of the individual to manage the heightened state of arousal without compromising performance or functioning and without exceeding the available resources of the individual (Lazarus and Folkman 1984). Coping is an adaptive response to a state of disequilibrium or distress. It is the ability to effectively manage stress within the range of expected demands of the situation (Suldo, Shaunessy and Hardesty 2008).

Stress may be triggered by new, novel, or unfamiliar situations, by situations which have previously been associated with stress and tension, by social and emotional situations, or by combinations of these factors. These situations may contain cognitive, sensory, social, emotional, behavioral, and physical elements, etc., where the individual is required to confront and respond to the situation in some manageable, effective, and adaptive ways. If the heightened arousal level is managed and controlled effectively, then equilibrium returns. Otherwise, stress will increase as the individual senses their vulnerability to the situation and their inability to control or manage effectively their heightened arousal level. This inability to manage or modulate stress levels may be related to a social competency deficit (the individual does not possess the ability or capacity to manage stress) or to a specific social skill deficit (the individual has some competency or ability to manage stress, but has limited specific skills to employ (i.e., is unable or unwilling to deal with the specific situation that arose). Each of these appears common in the ASD individual.

Anxiety is defined as a specific state of overarousal triggered by an internal or external situation (i.e., the stressor), creating stress (i.e., the stress response) which cannot be managed, controlled, or coped with in any effective way. Anxiety emerges as this state of increased stress and when effective management or coping strategies are unavailable to stabilize the individual or to reduce stress, thus resulting in stress overload, the state of anxiety. In most individuals, certain levels of stress and tension are a normal and frequent occurrence, requiring tolerance at lower levels and control, management, and adaptation (i.e., coping) at higher levels. While maintaining a general state of internal/external equilibrium is the preferred state for most individuals, managing and adapting to the frequent shifts in stress levels that regularly occur in the course of day to day experiences are necessary abilities. While these typically require a broad range of strategies and techniques, key components include: self-awareness, self-regulation, and self-monitoring; stress and anxiety management techniques; cognitive, behavioral, and emotional flexibility; and the use of external supports when needed and available.

For the individual with ASD, many of these strategies and techniques may not be consistently available to the individual or, when available, may be difficult to implement. For example, self-regulation/self-monitoring in a stress-free environment may occur relatively smoothly, but when an individual is contending with external change or disruption that results in increased internal stress states, self-regulation/self-monitoring mechanisms may operate less efficiently, whereupon the individual must rely upon additional combinations of stress/tension reducing mechanisms or contend with stress overload.

In the ASD individual, stress and tension appear to occur more frequently, more intensely, and with more adverse outcomes, particularly in social situations. There is some research support for the view that the majority of ASD and Asperger Disorder (AD) individuals may experience a social competency deficit in modulating arousal levels, particularly to social and sensory stimuli (Dawson 1991; Dawson and Lewy 1989; Kinsbourne 1987; Ornitz 1989), thus explaining the chronic states of stress/tension and anxiety that are observed and reported in new and unfamiliar situations by ASD individuals, particularly those involving social interactions or high levels of sensory input. These situations are likely to contribute to a circular pattern involving a sequence which includes social interaction, increased stress and tension, poor social response, increased stress, anxiety, etc. In other words, in the ASD individual, these concerns may each operate as triggers for one another, i.e., social interaction triggers stress, stress triggers anxiety, anxiety rises in relation to the demands of the social interaction; in an attempt to cope with the increased stress, tension, and anxiety, the social situation may be avoided. As a result, the ASD individual may need significantly more time to adapt or adjust to normal arousal levels prior to learning to cope with heightened arousal levels (i.e., learn to cope with "normal" stress) (Stevens and Gruzelier 1984).

Stress – understanding and coping with it

Understanding, anticipating, and managing stress are all critical aspects necessary for negotiating one's personal and social environments effectively. In the ASD individual, these issues can be complicated by problems specific to the disorder (i.e., innate social impairment) or by those exacerbated by the disorder (e.g., compulsive, repetitive behaviors). For example, social interactions, generally viewed as part of normal day to day existence, will likely produce some level of stress. Therefore when an ASD individual is in a group setting, issues and problems related to the stress experienced in interpersonal interactions are more likely to occur. These can be assessed in the real life experiences of the group with goals constructed and skills targeted immediately. Strategies and techniques for stress management can be taught, practiced and reinforced for use as necessary when problems arise within the group situation and then can be generalized to out of group experiences.

Cautious contentment

Over time, a number of consistent patterns have been observed in how individuals with ASD approach and manage potential stress producing situations. For most individuals, the absence of stress is associated with a state of calmness or in a state of relative equilibrium. The typical individual expects and anticipates some level of stress (heightened arousal) in moment to moment and day to day experiences and deals with these as they occur without significant disruption in one's overall state of relative equilibrium. For the ASD individual, this is described as a state of "cautious contentment," because this state appears to rely primarily upon the maintenance of "sameness and the avoidance of change," rather than being a dynamic, ongoing state of frequent adjustment and adaptation to change. In other words, the ASD individual strives to keep things from changing in order to avoid stress, whereas the typical individual "goes with the flow," adjusting to the minor changes that occur readily and fluidly without significant stress. At times, an individual may even encourage or seek out change to excite or arouse internal systems.

Many ASD individuals however, appear comfortable (i.e., at low/no stress levels) only when they are able to attain and maintain this state of "cautious contentment," which often includes the seeking out or repeating of known, repetitive situations and activities that are internally calming or relaxing for them. Frequently if not most often, these are solitary, isolated situations where they are in control, where sensory input is managed and controlled, where others do not intrude or try to change their situation, and when they can alter, change, or adjust their activities at their discretion as long as it maintains this state of "cautious contentment." To others, this may appear as existing with states of low arousal or the absence of arousal (i.e., no change), but for the ASD individual, it is managing, controlling, and maintaining their own state of arousal at tolerable levels.

These calming, relaxing tasks or situations become self-reinforcing and may be repeated over and over, becoming habituated, stereotypic, ritualized, and repetitive, in an effort to reconstruct and maintain the state of calm they are intended to induce. This range of behaviors and actions is viewed as serving to maintain a certain state of calm, anxiety-free, mostly self-created environments. These may be specific situations, i.e., playing with Lego, making up own games, reading, etc., or they may be specific repetitive and stereotypic play scenarios, i.e., repeating exactly the words to a book, reenacting a Star Wars battle exactly as created, repeating exactly a stepwise progression of activities to complete a game.

As long as the individual is allowed to recreate or to settle into these situations or tasks they will be quite easy to live with. However, the external environment is constantly making demands on every individual to relate, interact, respond, engage actively, and adapt to the environments that they must exist within. At home, parents and siblings will insist that they talk to them, relate to them, play with them, answer questions, and conform to demands and expectations, (e.g., get ready for bed, do homework, etc.). Compliance and cooperation with these demands is required to learn and understand the social experience of interaction with comfort and sustenance coming from the gratification, satisfaction and maintenance of connections and relationships that come with these interactions. In and of themselves, they become reinforcing of the benefits of social interaction and experience.

When ASD individuals are presented with external demands and expectations (from parents, siblings, peers, school, play), this appears to intrude upon and threaten their "cautious contentment," triggering a state of heightened alert and arousal and of potential disequilibrium. Typically, the individual attempts to adjust by "tightening up the barriers," essentially attempting to return to or reconstruct the state of equilibrium (calm/low stress) previously experienced. If the environmental stimulus continues to push the issue, two things are likely to occur, sending the situation toward a downward spiral; one, a movement toward increased stress-tension, and next, a shift toward increased rigidity/inflexibility.

When the individual's arousal level increases, increased stress and tension is triggered. While this is generally referred to as increased "anxiety," the true nature of the internal experience for the ASD individual is yet to be understood in order to precisely characterize this experience as discomfort, stress/tension, anxiety or just the experience of a difficult cognitive or emotional state. Nevertheless, external demands do change the internal dynamics of the situation for the individual. What may be a calm, relaxing, stress-free state while reading or playing quietly by oneself or constantly repeating a self-soothing tune as it plays on the CD player, is intruded upon by external demands, requiring change, alteration of the situation, intrusion by other individuals (peers or adults), or even requiring the individual to give up or abandon the task. The individual's heightened stress and tension triggers several reactions both by the individual to try and cope with and manage the situation and by the environment to cope with and manage a now stressed, "anxious," upset individual.

The Stress-Anxiety Continuum

As an individual experiences increasing states of arousal and stress, they will be confronted with "decisions" and "choices" as to how to cope with and manage the particular level of arousal of stress or anxiety. For some individuals, they will rapidly invoke effective and adaptive stress management strategies and techniques, thus preventing the development of increasing and spiraling stress and insuring a return to a level of equilibrium. For others, they may not possess adequate capacities to cope with or manage stress or anxiety effectively, and thus be unable to prevent increasing levels of stress and tension and the ongoing slide toward overload and meltdown.

The Stress-Anxiety Continuum provides a representation of specific states or levels of arousal along a continuum ranging from equilibrium to breakdown. At each point along the continuum, an individual makes "decisions" or "choices" as to how to best manage and deal with the stressful situation, event, or interaction that is occurring. These decisions or choices will differentiate between effective or adaptive coping and management strategies and ineffective and maladaptive management strategies. Various points along the Stress-Anxiety Continuum represent different levels of arousal each with multiple triggers and response patterns and with varying individual to individual thresholds which determine the degree and intensity of the response/reaction.

In this approach, stress is viewed as a function of increasing arousal levels associated with potential disequilibrium or distress, ultimately either being "managed" effectively or breaking through a stress threshold and moving to a higher level on the continuum. Stress, tension, and anxiety themselves are each complex concepts involving combinations of physiological, cognitive, social, and emotional components. While these components may occur in isolation, they are most likely to occur in multiple or overlapping combinations.

In individual and group experiences with ASD individuals, a range of responses and reactions to stress and tension producing situations have been observed. Some individuals appear capable of coping with low to moderate levels of stress efficiently and without further difficulty, while others experiencing the same levels of stress or tension will experience escalating levels of anxiety and often additional negative outcomes. Others still may be completely unable to manage even slight increases in anxiety and move quickly into a state of overload or "meltdown," where internal resources collapse and external resources cannot be accessed.

Based on experiences with ASD individuals using this approach, a majority of ASD individuals have reported and have been observed experiencing high baseline levels of stress/tension and anxiety. In those situations, even minor increases in stress will push through and exceed their manageable and tolerable threshold levels. While there is limited empirical data with ASD individuals which focuses specifically on the issue of stress, tension, and anxiety experiences or its components, the development and use of effective strategies for coping and management of these concerns as they arise with ASD individuals remains a critical endeavor.

The following progression along a continuum has been observed consistently with ASD individuals engaged in social interactions within group situations and appears particularly relevant to an understanding of the experience of stress, tension, and anxiety in ASD individuals. This progression along a Stress-Anxiety Continuum presents itself in the following ways:

Level 1 – Cautious contentment

Level 2 – Stress/tension

Level 3 – Anxiety

Level 4 – Overload

Level 5 – Breakdown

Figure 6.1 Stress-Anxiety Continuum

Pathway 1	Cautious contentment	Pathway 2
Effective management	(A state of relative equilibrium)	Ineffective management

-------------------------- Arousal threshold --------------------------

Stress – Tension

(A state of heightened arousal)

-------------------------- Stress-Tension threshold --------------------------

Anxiety

(A state of overarousal)

-------------------------- Anxiety threshold --------------------------

Overload

(Loss of cognitive, behavioral, or emotional control)

-------------------------- Overload threshold --------------------------

Breakdown

E
q
u
i
l
i
b
r
i
u
m

O
v
e
r
l
o
a
d

At each level, the individual is confronted with experiences, situations, and interactions which create a state of heightened arousal and which trigger a reaction (of coping/managing or of stress/tension, anxiety, or overload). These reactions may occur related to separate or to interacting experiences (e.g., physiological, cognitive, social, behavioral, emotional). At each level, there appear at least two clear pathways with one resulting in the evoking of management and coping strategies to sufficiently and effectively deal with, defuse, and control the experience within manageable levels resulting in decreased arousal. As this occurs, the individual gradually returns to a state of equilibrium and proceeds to move forward in normal ways.

The second pathway results from the inability to adequately or effectively manage the experience, situation, or interaction (increasing arousal levels), moving through threshold levels and resulting in a state of overload and ultimately breakdown. As thresholds are broken through and overload occurs, the individual loses significant cognitive and emotional control over internal states and external variables. At this point, if the individual is unable to evoke any useful or effective strategies or to rely on external controls in order for a state of equilibrium to be regained, then they will be unable to prevent an inevitable "meltdown" or breakdown.

In a best case scenario, the individual experiences stress or tension, recognizes the experience, and moves to manage and control it within threshold limits with no significant cognitive or emotional costs. In a worst case scenario, the individual experiences stress or tension which they are unable to effectively manage or control, resulting in escalation. This triggers a stress overload which in turn results in increasing levels of anxiety which trigger a range of cognitive, emotional, and physiological reactions. If these anxiety reactions are not managed, then increased escalation continues to the next level and cognitive and emotional thresholds are broken through, overload is triggered, then intensifies through thresholds and then ultimately meltdown (an "anxiety attack")/"breakdown" occurs where the individual is unable to access any effective management or coping strategies without external influence.

Stress-Anxiety assessment

Establishing the ASD individual's strengths and weaknesses relative to the management and control of stress, tension, and anxiety as it occurs along the Stress-Anxiety Continuum occurs next. In this context, prominent signs/signals, triggers, and responses to stress, tension, and anxiety are assessed in order to evaluate the individual's response for adaptability in social and group interactions, and to construct plans and interventions to serve a more adaptive response to the stress, tension, and anxiety that the ASD individual experiences. Information on the ASD individual's experience of stress, tension, and anxiety is collected from available data sources and observations is reported on the Individual Profile – Stress-Anxiety Assessment that is part of the Initial Evaluation and Interview Form (described in Chapter 12).

Figure 6.2 Individual Profile – Stress-Anxiety Assessment

Please code: Never – 1; Rarely – 2; Sometimes – 3; Often – 4; Always–5

		N	R	S	O	A
1.	Can recognize and acknowledge general situations that cause tension and stress	1	2	3	4	5
2.	Can recognize and acknowledge social situations that cause tension and stress	1	2	3	4	5
3.	Looks forward to new social situations and to meeting new people	1	2	3	4	5
4.	Warms up easily to a new environment	1	2	3	4	5
5.	Introduces self to unfamiliar peers	1	2	3	4	5
6.	Converses freely with others once introduced	1	2	3	4	5
7.	Shares information about self	1	2	3	4	5
8.	Appears comfortable and relaxed with peers in group situations	1	2	3	4	5
9.	Uses stress and anxiety management strategies	1	2	3	4	5
10.	Has a variety of stress and anxiety management strategies available	1	2	3	4	5
11.	Always manages to avoid overload	1	2	3	4	5
12.	Always manages to avoid meltdown/breakdown	1	2	3	4	5

Total score _____

Anxiety Assessment Scoring Continuum

	High stress/Anxiety		Moderate stress/Anxiety		Manages stress/Anxiety	
	Low coping/Management		Moderate coping/Management		Good coping/Management	
	—	—	—	—	—	
Scores	12	24	36	48	60	

From this information, individual goals can then be constructed which relate specifically to the needs of the ASD individual in the management and control of stress, tension, and anxiety (described in Chapters 11 and 12).

Next in this chapter, stress and anxiety control and management techniques are discussed, how they relate to stress and anxiety in ASD individuals, how they can be taught and learned within the group structure and process, and how they can be implemented effectively in group and peer interactions.

Stress and anxiety control and management

Stress and anxiety are pervasive and often debilitating factors in the day to day functioning of ASD individuals. It is particularly prominent in the social interactions of ASD individuals where attention to and understanding of another person's needs is vital to effective and satisfying social communication, but also significantly affected by the intrusion of stress, tension, and anxiety. The ASD individual will often be struggling to manage, cope with, and overcome deficits in all or some aspects of attention (especially joint attention), to understand the perspectives and views of others (theory of mind), to use pragmatic communications effectively (correctly interpreting verbal and nonverbal cues), and to use effectively aspects of cognitive and executive functioning (initiating, planning, organizing, self monitoring) and, at the same time, to manage high degrees of stress, tension, and anxiety.

In the process of social interaction, the ASD individual must learn to experience, recognize, monitor, and control the stress, tension, and anxiety that is typically evoked in social interactions. A group-focused, peer-based, and adult-monitored setting provides opportunities for social interactions and exchanges to take place in a safe and supportive environment where the primary goals for each group participant are to acknowledge that stress and anxiety are an inevitable aspect of social interaction, to recognize when these states are triggered for the individual, and to learn both individual and group-based strategies to effectively manage and cope with stress, tension, and anxiety, as well as their approach to threshold level, overload, and breakdown.

Within this approach, at each stage of group functioning, group participants are educated about how these issues may play out, are taught strategies and techniques to manage stress and anxiety effectively, and are given multiple opportunities to use and practice these skills in real-life, peer interactions. Following each stress/anxiety event, group discussion, processing, and debriefing can occur, together with priming of the group for the inevitable "next event."

The effective management of stress and tension, of approaches to threshold levels, of anxiety, and of overload, involves specific techniques which employ both cognitive and emotional control over a range of internally and externally generated stress and anxiety-producing reactions. These techniques address the range of reactions that may occur along the Stress-Anxiety continuum, beginning with initial experiences or interactions which create stress or tension, the building and escalating stress and tension which produce anxiety, anxiety reactions, and the poorly controlled anxiety responses which result in overload and breakdown.

Stress and anxiety control and management techniques should include aspects of both cognitive control and emotional control which can be brought to bear on reactions occurring anywhere along the Stress-Anxiety Continuum (see Figure 6.1). All individuals, including individuals with ASD, can be provided with training to recognize heightened arousal and stress signals and approaches to threshold levels and to manage, control, or prevent anxiety reactions. They can also learn to manage and cope with anxiety adequately and effectively when it occurs, and to recover from emotional overload and breakdown when necessary.

A key component at each stage of this group intervention focuses specifically on facilitating the management and regulation of stress and anxiety so that other group processes can proceed with less interference. Stress and anxiety prevention, control, and management are connected to all group goals and embedded within both early and later sessions of all groups through stress management and relaxation techniques. Stress management and self-calming techniques are geared toward the goals which help individuals manage stress when it arises, manage anxiety that is stress generated, and regain equilibrium and stabilization once overload and meltdown is approached.

Training in social competency and social skill building for each specific stress and anxiety control and management technique follows a consistent pattern and series of steps which include:

1. Group members are "educated" about the meaning of stress, tension, and anxiety and how, when, and why it occurs.

2. Group members are taught specific techniques at the appropriate points within each group stage and are given multiple practice opportunities.

3. Specific (first mild, then moderate) stress and anxiety producing situations are leader constructed and implemented, then managed, with the group then discussing, practicing, and debriefing what specific strategies and techniques would be most effective in the specific situation confronted.

4. The group as a whole participates in practicing the learned strategies and techniques in group constructed, play acted, and modeled situations.

5.   As naturally occurring stress and anxiety producing situations play out in the group, members are prompted to employ learned strategies and techniques appropriate for the specific situation and to share these experiences with their peers in group.

6.   Appropriate use of stress and anxiety control and management techniques is reinforced consistently.

The goal of this training is to effectively manage, cope with, and reduce levels of stress, tension, and anxiety by evoking states of increased calmness and decreased muscle tension and to increase self-awareness, and increased self-control. Primarily, techniques are employed which include relaxation, positive self-talk, and affective expression. These techniques fit within and complement a cognitive-developmental framework within a group psychotherapeutic approach.

Relaxation training

Group participants are provided with brief, simple, easy to learn, modified relaxation techniques sufficient to help them manage and cope with stress and tension as it arises in interactive group situations. Techniques provided and taught also focus on helping each individual learn useful stress management techniques which can be generalized for use with other stress-producing situations both within and outside of group. The focus is on specific stress and anxiety producing situations which will arise in group interactions. Group participants are provided in advance with training and practice through "priming" for the different types of interactions which are likely to occur within the group. Specific stress management techniques are then taught, reinforced, and practiced within group sessions and then embedded within ongoing and subsequent activities.

As the stress or anxiety producing situations emerge, stress and anxiety management techniques appropriate to the situation are directed into play by the group leader. Two relaxation techniques, deep breathing and progressive muscle relaxation, have been found easiest to learn and most beneficial for group participants with ASD using this approach. Both are passive relaxation exercise regimens which are quickly learned, easily self or other prompted and initiated, readily practiced, self-reinforcing, and generally imperceptible to others while being performed.

In initiating these techniques with ASD children during initial group situations, group members are encouraged to settle into a comfortable spot either standing, on a chair (e.g., a beanbag or cushioned chair), or on the floor within the group room, to close their eyes or to pick a point of focus, and to clear their head of any distracting or confusing thoughts. Then they begin with learning the following.

Deep breathing

The deep breathing technique involves learning to take long, slow breaths, lasting upwards of 4–10 seconds each, and drawing air into the diaphragm and abdominal area. The focus of each breath is shifted from the lungs in normal breathing to the diaphragm and emphasis is placed on the measured, slow, paced inhaling, pauses at the peak of intake, and slow, measured, and calm exhaling. Five to ten smooth and relaxed inhale–exhale cycles are generally sufficient once learned and practiced to significantly lower stress-tension levels to more manageable capacities.

Deep breathing is a basic, quick, efficient, and easy to learn relaxation technique that can be performed in any environment. The calming effects are immediate and with practice and repetition, these effects can be consistently enhanced and improved (Bourne 2005).

Progressive muscle relaxation

Progressive muscle relaxation, based on techniques developed by Jacobson (1974), involves the engaging of individual muscles or muscle groups in a cycle of tension-relaxation, taking 5–10 seconds each. The individual is taught to move systematically through a series of 10–20 muscle groups, each time tensing then relaxing the muscle or muscle group focused on and "learning" to recognize and mentally note the relaxation state of the muscles. Increased facility with progressive muscle relaxation allows the individual to select muscles and areas of tension for concentrated focus and relaxation efforts. Davis, Eshelman, and McKay (2000) provide a detailed description of this technique in its entirety and the adaptations described by Cautela and Groden (1978) for use with special needs children are useful for training ASD children in group situations.

While this particular technique requires more practice than deep breathing, many aspects of the learning process can be embedded within fun activities created specifically for young ASD children. As with deep breathing, progressive muscle relaxation can be employed as a quick and efficient stress and tension reducer, particularly when stress producing situations arise spontaneously within the group setting.

With both the deep breathing and progressive muscle relaxation techniques, it is helpful for ASD individuals to designate a "cue" or signal, that a relaxation, self-calming technique is required in the situation that is occurring at the moment. For example, the group leader may signal, "time to relax" or "time to calm" or "slow down time," etc., by a previously discussed hand gesture, a verbal cue (e.g., "deep breath," "inhale," "five seconds," etc.), a handy prescribed placard or index card, etc.

Positive self-talk

Self-talk is the label given to the internal monologue that accompanies various events, situations, and interactions that individuals encounter as they go through their lives. Some individuals constantly use this internal monologue as an attempt to sort out, understand, or talk through what they are experiencing. Others employ self-talk only episodically, such as when confused, anxious, excited, angry, or needing to generate alternatives to choose from. In work with ASD individuals, the term self-talk is employed in its most general and global way as an internal monologue, generating thoughts and feelings, falling on a fairly broad continuum from negative to positive.

Positive self-talk represents positive self-statements, self-affirmations, motivating factors, ego boosts, and esteem builders. With ASD individuals, it is best to address and reinforce only that subset of positive self-talk that represents reality-based interpretations by the individual. The subset of positive self-talk that represent any distorted, fantasy-based, unrealistic, or self-serving interpretations by the individual (e.g., "I'm smarter than you," "I am always happy") are typically ignored or subtly confronted (e.g., "Everyone is smart in this group," "Everyone has some down moments").

Training is provided to group participants in the appropriate use of positive self-talk through priming (e.g., "Think of the best thing that can happen in the game we are about to play"), modeling by group leaders (e.g., " You are working really hard"), rapid verbal reinforcement ("That was a great thing to say to J."), written scripts (e.g., "Let's generate a story about how our group helps J. fix his computer"), and generating scripted and repeated positive self-affirmations (both for each individual within the group and for the group as a whole). Throughout each session, group leaders closely attend to the verbal and body language of the participants, commenting, clarifying, or reinforcing the use of positive self-talk as the group proceeds through its tasks and activities.

Positive self-talk is considered a stress and anxiety management technique because of its effects in countering negative thoughts, distortions, and self-disparagement, that generate stress and tension and ultimately create or increase anxiety both for the individual and for the group. As these efforts are countered and neutralized, it allows group participants to learn how to extract and experience positive aspects of interactions to use as a foundation for an improved sense of self. Positive self-talk is known to enhance and reinforce this process (Helmstetter 1987).

Affective expression

Experiencing and expressing feelings and emotions as they occur has long been known to have calming and curative effects. While this process is not completely understood, it is believed that allowing individuals to give expression to feelings, emotions, and internal states, increases a sense of cognitive control over their current situation. Also, the expression of feelings and emotions to another individual opens the door for additional input into understanding and managing these feelings and emotions and in itself fosters an interactive, communication process. In this group-based approach, group participants are given structured opportunities to address both the situations and interactions that trigger stress (and to use the group members and group process for problem solving strategies) and the emotions aroused in stressful situations (through stress/tension control and management techniques).

In this approach, expressions of feelings, emotions, and internal states are viewed as potential stress and anxiety reducing techniques. In this group-based approach, the expression of feelings, emotions, and internal states are encouraged so that they can be explored and responded to in sensitive and helpful ways within the group experience. Attempts are consistently made to combine other stress and anxiety management techniques (deep breathing, muscle relaxation, positive self-talk) with affective expression so as to address the exact level of stress that may exist within the experience, connected to the feelings being described.

From the outset of all groups, appropriate affect expression is modeled by the group leader, is encouraged and reinforced when it occurs appropriately, and is reframed, redirected, or limited when expressed inappropriately. Specific verbal or written scripts are also provided and practiced when necessary. In this process, the importance of recognizing, experiencing, and expressing feelings, emotions, and internal states, is emphasized and that individuals can employ affective expression as a tool to manage and cope with stress, tension, and anxiety. Given the view here of these groups as therapeutically-based, affective expression, affective management, and cognitive control are also considered necessary components of the therapeutic process.

Given the prominent role that stress and anxiety plays in the interpersonal functioning of ASD individuals, strategies and techniques to manage these issues most effectively are considered critical and all groups are provided training, practice, and reinforcement of techniques best suited for their age and level of development. Discussion and practice are initiated during the first sessions and followed up in all subsequent Stage 1 sessions. During later stages, those techniques learned are called upon as needed for the specific situations that arise.

Chapter 7

Attention

It is generally believed and extensively reported that the majority of individuals with Autism Spectrum Disorders (ASD) demonstrate problems with attention and focus (e.g., Frith 1989; Rosenn 2002) with estimates as high as 60–70 percent of ASD children (Rosenn 2002). Asperger (1991) himself reported that the "disturbance of active attention" was common in those high functioning autistic children he observed. However, while there are few empirical studies which specifically address attention in ASD individuals, those completed consistently report evidence of attention deficits (Schatz, Weimer and Trauner 2002).

Available studies make clear that the underlying nature and source of these attentional concerns may vary within the ASD population. Frith (1989) has described attention in ASD individuals as varying between "overload" states where the individual is unable to attend to simultaneously presented information and "underload" states where the individual is unable to focus on any important piece of information. Either state results in faulty or inadequate attention. Similar results have been reported by others with the common finding of attention deficits in focused (Pierce, Glad and Schreibman 1997), sustained, selective (Frith and Baron-Cohen 1987; Lovaas, Koegel, and Schreibman 1979), flexible (Ciesielski, Courchesne and Elmasian 1990; Courchesne 1991), and joint (Wilczynski *et al.* 2007) attention. In fact, anecdotal and observational data suggest that in general, attention may be defined much too broadly and generically to be of value when attempting to address these problems in ASD individuals. Empirical studies to date have indicated that to address this problem precisely, the specific attentional variable must be explicitly and operationally defined for evaluation and measurement, then considered within the ASD individual's overall cognitive and learning style (Schatz *et al.* 2002).

It is believed that attention is a complex set of concepts rather than having a singe unitary meaning. Recent research into specific aspects of attention (Mirsky *et al.* 1991) indicates that attention is a cognitive/neurological function influenced and affected by many variables, but is also governed by underlying developmental components. The ability to employ attention appears dependent on a range of cognitive, neurological, constitutional, social-emotional, and even genetic variables. While theories of brain function, including neurological/neuropsychological functioning, hold great promise, in group-based interventions the challenge remains to understand, address, and remediate a range of different types of attention deficits that may emerge and influence the quality of social interactions.

In this approach, attention is viewed not as a single variable, but as a broad concept which includes several different types of attention. An ASD individual may demonstrate one or more specific types of attentional problems or deficits. The few available empirical studies indicate that the majority of ASD individuals exhibit some type of attentional problem or deficit (Rosenn 2002), but there are few studies that have separated attention into its specific components for subsequent study. Taking a developmental perspective, attention may be viewed as a broad category encompassing specific and overlapping aspects of: focused attention, sustained attention, selective attention, flexible attention, and joint attention (Figure 7.1).

Figure 7.1 Developmental progression of attention

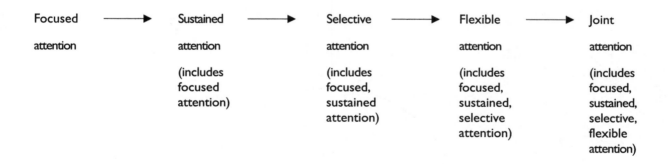

Focused attention → Sustained attention (includes focused attention) → Selective attention (includes focused, sustained attention) → Flexible attention (includes focused, sustained, selective attention) → Joint attention (includes focused, sustained, selective, flexible attention)

In this approach and based on observations and experiences with ASD individuals, an attempt is made to assess these five aspects of attention which appear important to the social interactive processes taking place within a peer-based, group-focused, cognitive-developmental model. While there may be other aspects of attention not included here, the variables chosen provide a way to address and assess these specific aspects of attention within this approach.

The five variables of attention addressed here include:

Focused attention – this is the ability to direct one's attention to a desired task or activity on demand by the individual and to hold it there for some minimal amount of time, as characterized in Figure 7.2.

Figure 7.2 Flow of focused attention

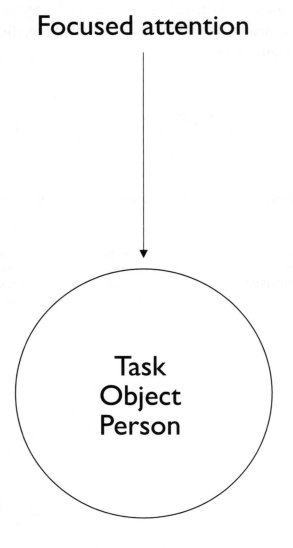

Sustained attention – this is the ability to hold and sustain one's attention to a desired task or activity over an extended period of time (as designated from Time 1 to Time 2) which is defined either by the individual or by the task. This is characterized in Figure 7.3.

Figure 7.3 Flow of sustained attention

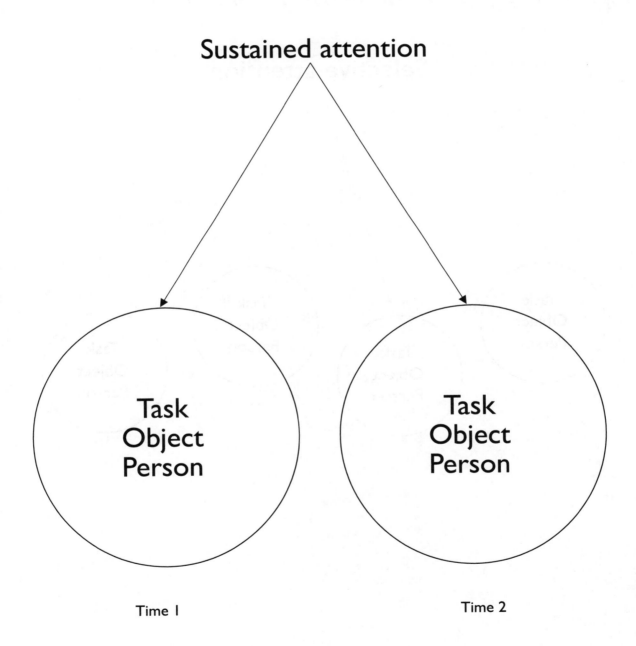

Selective attention – this is the ability to differentiate types of stimuli to be focused on and to selectively and purposefully direct attention to a task defined as relevant and important and to simultaneously withhold attention from other stimuli defined as irrelevant, unimportant, or distracting to the task currently focused on. This is characterized in Figure 7.4.

Figure 7.4 Flow of selective attention

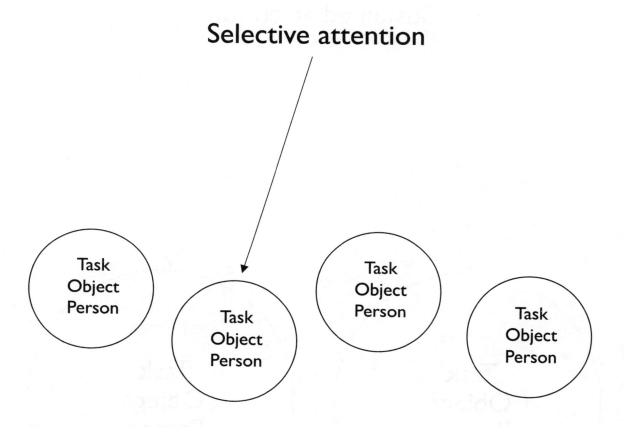

Flexible attention – this is the ability to flexibly and spontaneously shift attention from one task or activity to another task or activity without the prior task or activity disrupting focus or attention to the task or activity being shifted to. Flexible attention may at times involve multiple and frequent shifts of attention between two or more tasks or activities and is characterized in Figure 7.5.

Figure 7.5 Flow of flexible attention

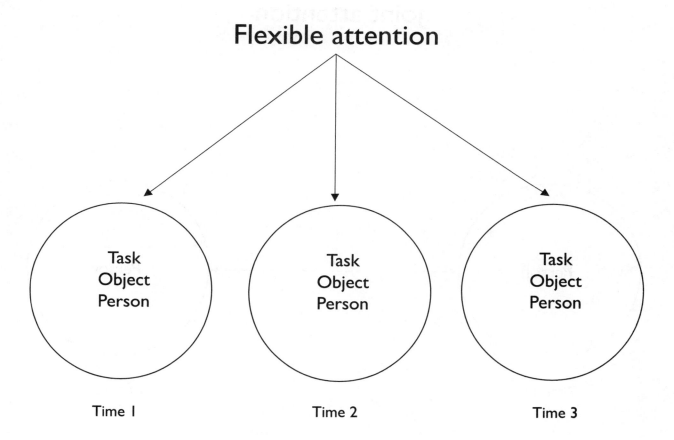

Joint attention – this is the ability to recognize and respond to the requests, demands, or needs for attention elicited by others. This joining with another person results in a mutual and reciprocal focus of attention on a particular experience, task, or activity. This is characterized in Figure 7.6.

Figure 7.6 Flow of joint attention

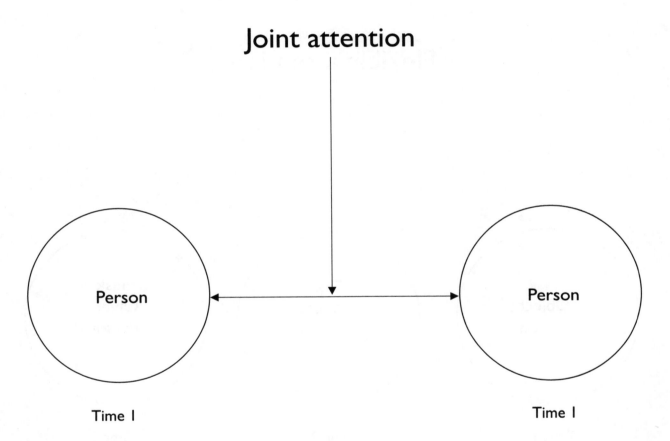

Although based on the limited research in this area, a developmental view of attention appears to begin with the inherent ability at birth of the child to locate and attend to stimuli of need, interest, and importance (i.e., the breast, mother's voice, light, etc.) with focused attention. Once able to focus attention on stimuli and objects of choice, the capacity to sustain that attention for increasing amounts of time develops, followed by the ability to attend selectively, that is, to specific aspects of available stimuli designated as important while ignoring other aspects considered irrelevant, contradictory, or distracting. Following the development of focused, sustained, and selective attention, comes the ability to spontaneously and flexibly shift attention to other stimuli, objects, or activities, deemed relevant or important, as internal or external factors dictate.

This developing capacity to flexibly shift attention between tasks or stimuli assumes the capacity to focus and direct attention at will, to sustain that attention on a task for some period of time sufficient to complete the task, and to focus and sustain attention on a specific selective task, withdrawing or withholding attention from other stimuli that might command attention. The capacities to focus, sustain, selectively attend, and flexibly shift attention, all appear necessary components of the most developmentally complex aspect of attention, that is, joint attention.

Joint attention is the capacity to direct and employ attentional capacities as they relate to shared interpersonal requirements and expectations. Joint attention is the mutual recognition of shared and reciprocal interaction that makes significant demands on each individual involved. It involves eye gaze, gestures, verbal and nonverbal cues in the presence of related and relevant input from others (Wilczynski *et al.* 2007). To recognize, understand, and respond to these demands in an interpersonal interaction requires each of the developmental components of attention, moving from focused attention through to joint attention. Several studies have addressed the issue of joint attention in ASD individuals and consistently found deficits that inhibit or impede social interactions and shared experiences (Loveland and Landry 1986; Sigman *et al.* 1986; Wilczynski *et al.* 2007).

Because attention is viewed as following a developmental trajectory, each individual considered for group placement is evaluated during the intake and assessment phase for their specific attentional capacities (described in Chapter 12). Individual goals are then created based on the presence and absence of these capacities. Information is collected from previous evaluations and reports, parent/caretaker data and observations, and interview interactions and observations. This information is then used to complete ratings (1–5; low–high) for each of the five attention variables and together with relevant examples of behavior observed are recorded on the Individual Profile – Attention Assessment which is one part of the Initial Evaluation and Interview Form. If then placed within a group, group goals and related group activities are formulated based on the attentional capacities and needs of each individual within the group, including their highest level of attention attained and demonstrated in consistent fashion.

Figure 7.7 Individual Profile – Attention Assessment

Focused attention

Please code: Never – 1; Rarely – 2; Sometimes – 3; Often – 4; Always – 5

		N	R	S	O	A
1.	Can locate items, objects, or people in environment at will	1	2	3	4	5
2.	Can choose a task or activity when many choices are available	1	2	3	4	5
3.	Can recognize different aspects of tasks/activities that are focused on	1	2	3	4	5
4.	Attends to name being called	1	2	3	4	5

Total score _____

Sustained attention

Please code: Never – 1; Rarely – 2; Sometimes – 3; Often – 4; Always – 5

		N	R	S	O	A
5.	Can complete more than one step of a multistep task	1	2	3	4	5
6.	Stays with tasks for extended periods of time	1	2	3	4	5
7.	Can complete all steps of a multistep task of choosing	1	2	3	4	5
8.	Can complete all steps of multistep task when directed by others	1	2	3	4	5

Total score _____

Selective attention

Please code: Never – 1; Rarely – 2; Sometimes – 3; Often – 4; Always – 5

		N	R	S	O	A
9.	Focuses on tasks of interest with other things going on around him/her	1	2	3	4	5
10.	Ignores peripheral stimuli or distractions when task focused	1	2	3	4	5
11.	Can redirect self to important activities when pulled off task	1	2	3	4	5
12.	Spontaneously recognizes and focuses on most relevant tasks at hand	1	2	3	4	5

Total score _____

Figure 7.7 Individual Profile – Attention Assessmet cont.

Flexible attention

Please code: Never – 1; Rarely – 2; Sometimes – 3; Often – 4; Always – 5

		N	R	S	O	A
13.	Tolerates shifts, changes, and transitions with significant stress	1	2	3	4	5
14.	Follow directions of others for shifts, changes, or transitions	1	2	3	4	5
15.	Initiates shifts from one task or activity to another without rigidity	1	2	3	4	5
16.	Upon direction of others, easily moves from one task to another	1	2	3	4	5

Total score   _____

Joint attention

Please code: Never – 1; Rarely – 2; Sometimes – 3; Often – 4; Always – 5

		N	R	S	O	A
17.	Locates people of interest to him/her	1	2	3	4	5
18.	Initiates exchanges with others	1	2	3	4	5
19.	Recognizes and responds to verbal/nonverbal (social) cues from others	1	2	3	4	5
20.	"Engages" or connects with others in reciprocal ways	1	2	3	4	5

Total score   _____

Attention Assessment Scoring Continuum (for each individual area)

	Low attention		Moderate attention	Excellent attention	
	-------	-------	-------	-------	-------
Scores	4	8	12	16	20

Attention Assessment Scoring Continuum – Total score

	Low attention		Moderate attention		Excellent attention
	-------	-------	-------	-------	-------
Scores	20	40	60	80	100

Chapter 8

Flexibility, Change, and Transition

Cognitive and behavioral flexibility is defined here as the capacity to cope with, manage, and adapt to changes, shifts, and transitions, as they occur within one's personal and interpersonal environments (i.e., internal or external) and as they alter the demands and expectations placed upon the individual.

From it earliest description, the insistence on sameness, resistance to change, and behavioral inflexibility have been defining characteristics of Autism Spectrum Disorder (ASD) (Kanner 1973) and have been consistently linked to social impairment (Berger *et al.* 1993; McEvoy, Roger and Pennington 1993; Szatmari *et al.* 1989; Wing and Gould 1979). Thus, in order to facilitate engagement in appropriate social interactions, a critical issue arises around the ASD individual's inability to engage the world, especially the social interpersonal world, in flexible ways. The issue of flexibility appears to have its origins in neurological (Delis, Kaplan, and Kramer 1999; Lezak 1995) and cognitive (Klein 1970) processes, with the outcome manifested in either or both of cognitive and behavioral inflexibility or rigidity. This issue also appears to have a strong relationship and connection to flexible attention processes although there is limited research to date in this area.

With ASD individuals, Flannery and Horner (1994) assert that increased rigidity may reflect a need for predictability (i.e., sameness) and when joined with the ASD individual's lack of awareness of surrounding informational cues signaling the need for change, characteristic restrictive and stereotypic patterns of behavior may arise. When change was made more predictable (i.e., signaled), problem behaviors were reduced. Similarly, increased availability of adult interaction (Kern and Vorndran 2000), increased contingent attention (Repp and Karsh 1994), and manipulation of environmental variables (Sterling-Turner and Jordan 2007), also appear to reduce the intensity of inflexibility/rigidity when change is introduced.

Antecedent intervention techniques also have demonstrated positive effects in reducing inflexibility/rigidity in both individual and group situations and have been employed successfully in a variety of group therapeutic situations. These include signaling change (Flannery and Horner 1994), verbal prompts (Tustin 1995), auditory inputs (Ferguson *et al.* 2004), behavioral momentum (Singer, Singer, and Horner 1987), visual inputs (Schmit *et al.* 2000), physical guidance, activity schedules (Dettmer *et al.* 2000), and videotape modeling (Schreibman, Whalen, and Stahmer 2000).

In social competency training and social skills instruction, a primary goal is to foster and encourage an increased flexibility in thinking, behaving, and interacting with other individuals and with the environment since inflexibility and rigidity are known to reduce the quality and quantity of an individual's interactions with the world around them. Behaviors involving inflexibility/rigidity as manifested by ASD individuals may include isolation, noncompliance, aggression, stereotypic movements or activities, transition problems, and tantrums. These difficulties may ultimately limit the ASD individual's independence.

With ASD individuals, requirements for cognitive and behavioral flexibility, change, and transitions, are often reported to result in a state of increased internal tension, often labeled in the literature as an increase in "anxiety," but best described here as a state of heightened arousal. This is based on an understanding of cognitive and behavioral rigidity as a response to a request or demand for change, causing a heightened state of arousal, triggering increased tension, and creating a state of disequilibrium or distress. If the individual is unable to manage or cope effectively (i.e., make the adjustment) and regain equilibrium, then stress and tension will continue to increase. In many situations, cognitive and behavioral inflexibility appears to be an attempt to maintain a preferred state of equilibrium actively initiated by the individual as a reaction to the increased stress and tension created by demands for change, shifts, or transitions.

Demands or requirements placed on the ASD individual for flexibility, change, or transition, are likely to heighten arousal and trigger movement along the Stress-Anxiety Continuum (as discussed in Chapter 6), resulting in either the invoking of coping and adaptation strategies or in progression toward overload. When unable to manage or cope with a situation requiring change or flexibility, the individual moves from a state of internal equilibrium, prior to a request or requirement for change, to a heightened state of arousal or disequilibrium after a change request is made. This change in state triggers stress and tension with the anticipated or approaching situation (change). The individual attempts to regain equilibrium and to reduce the tension being created by remaining at (or returning to) the previous (preferred) state of (lower) arousal (a state of cautious contentment), solely by remaining involved in the same task or activity with no consideration for other alternatives. This attempt to return to a state of cautious contentment (lower arousal/equilibrium) by the ASD individual does not serve as an adaptive strategy to manage stress or tension, but rather as part of a more fixed and rigid system to maintain equilibrium through "sameness." Thus in a change situation involving the ASD individual, they move from a state of perceived calm to a state of increased tension, triggering a state of inflexibility/rigidity in the hope of returning to the preferred state of calm (sameness). When the external environment cannot or will not comply with the individual's attempts to maintain the status quo and pushes for further change, then "stress" behaviors for the individual are likely to emerge (e.g., isolation, refusal, noncompliance, anger/aggression, tantrums) as manifestations of the individual's altered internal state, that is, a state of increased stress/tension and state of heightened arousal. Given the fixed and rigid qualities to this sequence, overload and meltdown are often inevitable cognitive and behavioral outcomes.

In the group-based approach described here, the attempts to help ASD individuals manage these states, which are likely to differ from individual to individual, are multifaceted. First, attempts are made to help the individual manage their stress and tension, not by a solution of inflexibility/rigidity, but by first reducing tension in order to allow the individual to reconsider their options, usually with previously learned stress and anxiety control and management techniques. Second, we attempt to intersperse into the situation demands that have a positive reinforcing capacity and a high likelihood of compliance, further reducing the individual's tension state. This intervention, characterized as behavioral momentum (Nevin 1996), has been shown to increase compliance during change situations (Ray, Skinner, and Watson 1999; Romano and Roll 2000; Singer *et al.* 1987). Third, interventions with ASD individuals that approach the problem from a number of different directions are considered, depending on the individual's involved, the group makeup, and the specific individual and group goals that might apply. This is considered a key aspect of the specific individual and group goal-oriented approach used in this approach (described in Chapter 12).

Inflexibility/rigidity presents as one of the defining characteristics of ASD as their rigid adherence to routines, rules, and restrictive, repetitive, and stereotypic patterns of behavior, and preoccupations often dictate many aspects of their life. Frequently, there is a rigid adherence to sameness and lack of variation in a variety of categories. While these issues are most often viewed and considered related to a general concept of cognitive and behavioral flexibility/rigidity, we have found some distinctions between individuals diagnosed with Autistic Disorder (AD) and those diagnosed with other Pervasive Developmental Disorders (PDD).

When preliminary data was collected on both AD and Pervasive Developmental Disorder – Not Otherwise Specified (PDD-NOS) groups of children prior to and following social competency/social skill intervention, it was found that AD individuals tended to respond with inflexibility primarily around the behaviors of others as it impacted on them (e.g., another individual also using the Lego they were using) and secondarily around interruptions to what they were doing (e.g., "Time to turn off the Gameboy," "Now it's time for math"). In contrast, PDD individuals tended to respond with inflexibility primarily to difficulties and frustrations with inanimate objects (e.g., a toy not working, something they are using breaks) and secondarily to changes in routine (e.g., they are provided a different snack, an expected meeting is cancelled). We believe that this data provides some indication of qualitative differences in the response patterns between diagnostic groups and that the concept of flexibility/rigidity may be a broad term with multiple aspects and subgroupings. Thus, the subgroupings may cluster differently depending on diagnostic and other variables. However at this time, due to the limited information available on the concept of flexibility/rigidity between groups of PDD, ASD, AD, and High Functioning Autism (HFA) individuals, the broadest perspective is taken when considering flexibility/rigidity with ASD individuals.

The following are examples of tasks requiring flexibility that have been observed to trigger reactions of inflexibility/rigidity in ASD individuals. Generally, these are actions or behaviors initiated by others or in the external environment and when the ASD individual appears to be in a state of cautious contentment.

Object movement (e.g., "I'm going to move this over here"). This involves another individual disrupting a certain order or sequence constructed by the ASD individual.

Attention shift (e.g., "I need you to stop that and answer my question"). This involves a request for a shift in focus requiring flexible attention capacities.

Task change (e.g., "I need you to come to the table now"). This involves flexible attention, mental shifting, and acceptance of change.

New information (e.g., "Today, we are going to do things a little different"). This involves the introduction of new, unknown, or unfamiliar tasks requiring change or transition.

Sensory inputs (e.g., more confined space/louder noise levels than usual). This requires focused and selective attention capacities involving primarily sensory inputs and stimuli.

Consistency/sameness (e.g., "You cannot do that today/anymore"). This involves a task transition from a preferred activity to another (often non-preferred) activity.

Activity interruption (e.g., "Just listen to me for a minute"). This requires cognitive or behavioral delay (i.e., "Stop!"), flexible and joint attention, additional information processing (i.e., the task request), and decision making.

Regarding movement along an flexibility/rigidity continuum, ASD individuals appear to follow a path of: comfort zone/cautious contentment; a stimulus event, typically requiring change, transition, or adjustment which triggers stress/tension; marked increases in stress/anxiety occur; attempts are made to return to the original stimulus or original state of equilibrium (e.g., comfort zone/cautious contentment); repeated, often perseverative, attempts are made (even when unsuccessful) to return to the original state of equilibrium; further increases in stress/tension, resulting in anxiety states, may occur until thresholds are broken through and overload occurs; inflexibility/rigidity to alternative tasks presented may occur along with resistance, and sustained anxiety. Thus, the requirement for change will occur as follows:

Figure 8.1 Patterns of inflexibility/rigidity

External change/external triggers

Increased stress/anxiety

Individual assesses expectation for flexibility/change and personal willingness for flexibility/change and moves to one of the following:

Most adaptive

- Immediate and cooperative adjustment to change
- Excitement and stimulation with change
- Exaggerated rule following

Somewhat adaptive

- Quick adaptation with little thought to change, its meaning, or it consequences
- Slow adaptation with hesitation and reluctance, but eventual compliance
- Alternative approaches

Least adaptive

- Repetitive, perseverative attempts to reduce stress/ anxiety with refusal to change
- Repetitive, perseverative attempts to return to status quo with refusal to change
- Avoidance of new stimulus
- Become overwhelmed

In approaching the issue of flexibility, change, and transition, attempts are made to apply the following in individual and group goal setting and in task construction within the group:

1. predictability in upcoming tasks, unique situations, and transitions

2. signaling, preparation, and priming used as upcoming changes and transitions approach

3. consistent use of: verbal cues, auditory cues, behavioral momentum techniques, visual supports, and activity schedules.

Finally, it is most helpful and most highly reinforcing to pay close attention to how each individual responds to particular kinds of information regarding change and adjustment within the group and the stress it may induce, then providing that individual with specific strategies and techniques that can be used to effectively manage the situation. Also, regarding interactions and responses within the group situation, attention to other related variables, such as how many individuals are involved, the number and sequence of steps in a task, the length of a task, the nature of the activity, the degree of choice making, and the extent of involvement required by other group members, are important factors in moving ASD individuals toward more flexible and resilient response patterns.

In this group-based intervention, the specific techniques and interventions used within the group to address coping and management strategies for the key issue of flexibility, change, and transition, are initially dictated by information received through detailed developmental histories, reports of test functioning, behavioral observations, and completion of parent/caretaker and teacher social competency checklists, including information regarding the flexibility, change, and transition variables recorded on the Individual Profile – Flexibility, Change, and Transition Assessment which is one part of the Initial Evaluation and Interview Form (described in Chapter 12).

Figure 8.2 Individual Profile – Flexibility, Change, and Transition Assessment

Please code: Never – 1; Rarely – 2; Sometimes – 3; Often – 4; Always – 5

		N	R	S	O	A
1.	Does not require significant preparation and predictability for small or moderate changes or transitions	1	2	3	4	5
2.	Can tolerate change and transition with external structure	1	2	3	4	5
3.	Tolerates changes to preset plans and schedules without help	1	2	3	4	5
4.	Suggests alternatives when personal plans/suggestions thwarted	1	2	3	4	5
5.	Adjusts easily to any change or transition or alteration in plans	1	2	3	4	5

Total score

Flexibility, Change, and Transition Assessment Scoring Continuum

	High inflexibility		Moderate inflexibility		High flexibility
	Low capacity for change or transition		Moderate capacity for change or transition		Good capacity for change and transition
	------	------	------	------	------
Scores	5	10	15	20	25

Each individual considered for group placement will be evaluated based on this information obtained during the intake and assessment phase for their specific flexibility, change, and transition needs and capacities with subsequent individual goals created and based on these capacities. If then placed within a group, goals specific to the individual are then constructed in this area based on this information and ultimately combined with individual goal information of other individuals to form sets of group goals, focusing on behaviors emphasizing flexibility and using modeling, rehearsal and feedback, practice and repetition, and integration with other process and skill variables (e.g., anxiety/stress management and reduction).

Chapter 9

Managing and Regulating Affective and Emotional Responses

The effective management and regulation of affective and emotional responses as they arise in social situations involves a complex set of interrelated cognitive, information processing (neurological), emotional, behavioral, and social variables. This includes an accurate understanding of the situation one is confronted with, a varied repertoire of responses available for that situation, the selection of an appropriate response for that situation, and the effective implementation and follow through with that response as the situation dictates. These requirements apply to most personal and interpersonal situations that an individual confronts on a day to day basis.

The emphasis here is on those individuals with Autism Spectrum Disorder (ASD) who struggle with affective and emotional responses as they relate to social interactions and social situations. This includes processing and understanding of incoming information relating to the situation at hand (inputs), the formulating and selecting of an appropriate response, and the implementing of a response appropriately based on the environmental and social cues available (outputs). In helping ASD individuals appropriately address and manage affective and emotional responses in social situations, this approach attempts to provide a structured, safe, and supportive, peer-based environment where issues and concerns related to understanding, managing and regulating, and expressing affects and emotions can be addressed. Within a safe and supportive peer-based group, emotional risk-taking, constructive feedback, implementation of peer suggestions, and self-managed emotional monitoring are encouraged and reinforced. Issues of stress, anxiety, frustration, and anger are anticipated and are addressed and specific strategies to manage these emotions effectively are taught, as well as relying on peers to help and support this process.

Understanding the social situation

Within the group situation, group participants are provided a structure where they will experience different types of interactions (e.g., meeting unfamiliar individuals, sharing information about oneself, gathering information about others, confronting and resolving conflict with peers, feeling stressed and anxious, saying goodbye and experiencing loss, etc.), each of which stir up a range of feelings and emotions that are pointed out to group members, are addressed directly, and are discussed, processed, and understood. The group leader maintains a focus on the feelings and emotions surrounding specific situations by constructing tasks and activities which are stage-based and which focus on specific interactive situations.

In this way, group members will proceed through stage-based social situations, being confronted with and learning about the feelings and emotions connected to these situations. Group members are taught to recognize and experience the feelings and emotions associated with specific social situations (e.g., choosing a peer to team up with, confronting an obstinate peer, savoring the successful completion of a difficult group activity, etc.). Of particular focus in this approach is the recognition and awareness of situations involving key variables and core deficits for the ASD individual of stress, tension, and anxiety, attentional demands, and needs for flexibility, adjustments, and transitions.

Group participants are taught that as part of a group working on developing, maintaining, and improving the quality of their social interactions and social relationships, they will inevitably be faced with situations where stress and tension will occur, anxiety and overload will be triggered, the need for a range of attentional capacities will be required, and the need for flexibility and accommodation to change requirements and expectations will be confronted. It is in this context of addressing key variables and core deficits of ASD that individuals will not only learn and rely on strategies and techniques that directly address stress/tension/anxiety, attentional difficulties, and inflexibility/rigidity, but will also acknowledge and address the importance of their affective and emotional experiences and reactions in these situations.

Having a repertoire of responses available

As group members become more aware of and capable of recognizing and addressing feelings and emotions as part of the social interactive process, they are taught strategies and techniques to manage these feelings and emotions in effective, sensitive, and respectful ways. Group members are encouraged to apply the stress and anxiety control and management techniques, joint attention approaches, and flexibility and change strategies, previously learned in group, to these situations where feelings and emotions emerge and must be dealt with. Group discussions are ongoing about what strategies may be employed and are best for different situations. Members are encouraged to problem solve as a group in the search for new or additional ways to effectively manage and regulate feelings and emotions.

Within the group structure, individuals are encouraged to focus upon and improve capacities to focus and sustain attention within the peer interactions taking place and to actively participate in sharing and explaining thoughts, ideas, feelings, and emotions within the solution-focused environment. As cohesiveness is attained, the group participants are encouraged to actively engage one another, to learn when and how to respectfully confront one another, and to view each group session as a shared experience. Group members are expected to learn about one another, to guide each other in the consideration of problems and their solutions, and to support each other during times of stress. As problems are approached, group members facilitate the explaining of the range of available alternatives and possibilities and encourage more flexible approaches to problem solving.

Choosing the appropriate response for the situation

With increased awareness of the emergence of feelings and emotions in group situations and with training and practice in basic management strategies and techniques, the group members are encouraged to consider and attempt the application of different strategies when emotions arise and must be managed. These attempts are discussed and processed and members are encouraged to develop their own "toolbox" of strategies for the management and regulation of their own feelings and emotions as they might arise in group interactive and social situations.

Following through using the right tool for the situation

As the group proceeds through progressive stages, a range of different social situations are confronted and must be managed together with the coinciding feelings and emotions. Group members are taught to recognize the situation and its components (cognitive, social, emotional, behavioral), to choose a way to manage the situation, to implement the strategy, and to evaluate the success and benefits for the individual and the group. As these situations emerge, they are discussed and processed and additional strategies may be considered. The group is encouraged to work together to formulate a "group approach" as well as to support each individual group member in their struggles to find effective strategies to manage and regulate their feelings and emotions. At each step, the group leader prepares and primes the group to anticipate the next level of stress, attentional issue, and flexibility concern that is likely to emerge as the group proceeds through stages of development.

In this group-based approach where emphasis is placed on addressing underlying key process variables and core deficits and improving specific social skill development within a cognitive-developmental framework, aspects of emotional development, related to management, control, and regulation, can be addressed.

This approach follows a stepwise progression in focusing on these needs through:

1. raising awareness about affects and emotions: what they are, how they are experienced, and what forms of expression they may take

2. learning strategies and techniques to personally manage, control, and regulate one's own affects and emotions

3. learning how to recognize, experience, and use affects and emotions in interactions with peers, such as group-based situations

4. learning how to use one's increased awareness and understanding of affects and emotions to help others who may be struggling with their own management and control of affects and emotions.

In this approach, a strong emphasis is placed on providing ongoing opportunities for group participants to express and address affects and emotions as they arise in social interactions and particularly as they relate to the key process variables and core deficits that ASD individuals experience and struggle with. As previously discussed, key variables and core deficits, such as stress and anxiety control and management, attentional capacities, and flexibility/transitions, are directly addressed using cognitive-behavioral techniques within a group therapeutic setting that allows and encourages the expression, management, and discussion of affects and emotions as they arise within social interactions and social relationship building.

Chapter 10

Combining Social Competence and Social Skill Building

Social competence

The ability to recognize and respond appropriately to a social situation defines human interaction. For individuals with Autism Spectrum Disorder (ASD), it is this core deficit in social interaction that undermines their ability to understand and to relate to others in appropriate and expected ways. In this approach, social competence is defined as a complex combination of cognitive, social, and emotional abilities which come together as a social situation or social interaction arises. It consists of the sets of abilities that make up an individual's "social intelligence" and that allow an individual to learn and acquire sets of social skills to use in social interactions.

For example, when an individual walking down the street is approached and addressed by another individual, a social situation has emerged and presented itself, calling upon the social competence of both individuals. How do they each assess and view the situation (positive/negative)? Do they know or recognize each other? Is there history to the interaction? What social skills do each possess? Are they lonely, busy/rushed, preoccupied, overwhelmed, upset/angry, etc.? The social competence or social abilities of each individual will provide them with the capacity to recognize and understand the nature of the situation. The social skills possessed by each individual will allow them to consider and formulate responses to the complex set of interactions (verbal and nonverbal) that may follow.

Key underlying capacities or variables determine the level of social competence attained by each individual and will become factors in how this situation is experienced and understood by each individual. Will one or both individuals be stressed or anxious about the interaction (emotional variables)? Will one or both be able to recall important information about a previous interaction (e.g., name, last time seen, etc.) (cognitive variables)? And will one or both engage in the proper or polite greeting (social variables)?

In this situation, it can be seen how social competence is a function of the combined cognitive, social, and emotional capacities to adapt and engage in a spontaneous, socially acceptable, and mutually satisfying social interaction. In this way, social competence consists of the abilities to recognize, understand, and engage in a social interchange. The elements of social competence also provide an individual with sufficient capacities to acquire, learn, and implement sets of social skills necessary for successful and mutually rewarding, reciprocal social interchanges. Social competencies may include broad areas of functioning or they may be defined quite narrowly. Examples of broad social competencies (or structure or process) include: stress and anxiety control and management; attention; flexibility; relatedness; self-control/self-management; and theory of mind. Examples of narrowly defined social competencies (or structure or process) include: anxiety around meeting unfamiliar individuals; focused attention, sustained attention, selective attention, flexible attention, joint attention; memory for faces; and eye contact.

Social skills

While social competence relates to the underlying abilities or capacities for social interchange (e.g., attention to another individual, anxiety management, etc.), social skills are the sets of learned and acquired behaviors that allow individuals to "complete" a social interaction successfully. The implementation of social skills follows from the level of social competence the individual has attained. In the socially competent individual, the social interaction is perceived and understood accurately. In the socially competent individual, specific learned and acquired skills are employed in the social interchange, based on the individual's competence to read and "understand" the situation and on the individual's possession of a range of social skills to employ in any given situation.

Social skills may also refer to a broadly defined set of general skills or may be more narrowly and precisely defined. Examples of broadly defined social skills (more often these are sets of skills) include: conversational skills; listening skills; attending to verbal and nonverbal signals; and using facial expressions. Examples of more narrowly defined social skills include: saying hello; shaking hands; asking permission; waiting your turn; and acknowledging another's feelings.

The socially competent individual possesses:

1. the abilities to recognize, understand, and engage in a social interaction, and

2. sufficient learned and acquired social skills to successfully engage another individual and to "complete" a mutually reciprocal, mutually gratifying interaction with that individual.

Planning for social competence and social skill development

In attempting to address the remediation or management of deficiencies in social competence, it is necessary to first assess the social competence of the individual in order to gain an understanding of what social abilities exist and which are absent or deficient. This information is considered together with information on the extent to which the individual manages key variables necessary for social interaction with specific attention to those often lacking in ASD individuals (core deficits). With information related to an individual's social competence (social abilities) and functioning on key variables (core deficits of ASD), a plan for social skill development can be constructed and implemented within a group-based, peer-focused, stage-based, cognitive-developmental framework. This plan begins with the collection of "areas of interest" from information provided by parents, teachers, and observers of the individual in social situations. Areas or topics of interest typically fall into two broad, but separate categories: those relating to underlying process, structure, or competency variables (typically in the ASD literature, their absence is referred to as "core deficits") and those relating to specific skill or function variables (a more common designation often including both process and skill variables). Areas or topics of interest are designated based on the needs of the individual as they relate to social-interpersonal functioning and as they are expected to occur within group and interpersonal situations. They are gleaned from information provided during the initial intake and evaluation process and collected from parents, teachers, and previous evaluators and providers. They relate specifically to areas of deficit or deficiency that undermine effective social interaction and that will be necessary for successful completion of social interchanges.

Areas of interest for an ASD individual may include any combination of social competencies and social skills deemed of importance by parents, teachers, professional evaluators, and interviewers. Typically, areas of interest will be those recognized as important by multiple members of the ASD individual's team. These areas of interest will form the basis for the construction of individual goals. As individuals are considered for group participation, group participants are selected based on their similar areas of interests, both in terms of social competencies and social skills.

Next, individual goals are constructed based on the individual's areas of interest. If subsequently placed in a group, the individual goals of all the participants are reviewed together and specific group goals are formulated, typically in a process that involves all group members during initial group sessions.

During these initial sessions, group members are provided an understanding of how their individual and group goals relate to specific social competencies and how they impact one's understanding of social situations. Group participants are also provided an understanding of the importance of specific skills, what situations they are important and necessary for, and how to implement these specific skills. This will occur within the group through discussion, group leader or peer modeling, role-play, direct instruction, group leader and group member feedback, and reinforcement of specific target behaviors.

General social competence and social skill building techniques

General training in the building of social competencies and of social skills follows a consistent pattern and set of steps which include:

An area or topic of interest is introduced with a "topic plan" for how it will be addressed in group. This includes providing group members with a preview of what will be expected of them as the group addresses the topic and some discussion occurs of the specific tasks involved, of specific leader and group member roles, the expected benefits, some likely problems, and the desired outcomes.

Group members are provided information ("are educated") about the topic or area of interest, how it affects the group, what its meaning and purpose may be, and how it may occur in negative and in positive ways.

Specific techniques that address the area or topic are discussed and their suitability, individual fit, and group appropriateness are considered. Group decisions are made about what techniques and strategies will be most beneficial and useful in addressing the particular area or topic of interest.

Group members are taught specific techniques and provided multiple practice opportunities that address the specific area or topic of interest.

The group as a whole participates in practicing the learned strategies and techniques in group constructed, play acted, and modeled situations.

Specific situations which address the particular topic or area are constructed by the group leader and implemented within the flow of the group.

The group discusses and debriefs what strategies and techniques are most effective in the specific situation confronted.

As naturally occurring situations play out in the group, these are brought to group participant's attention and they are prompted to employ learned strategies and techniques appropriate for the specific situation.

Appropriate use of these techniques is reinforced consistently.

At present, the research on the effectiveness of social skills approaches is variable and inconsistent. This is due in part to the lack of agreement on what constitutes core social skills, to variation between different social skill curriculums, and to the lack of valid measures to assess the presence and absence of social skills. It is also due to the wide variation in research design when these issues are addressed, including differences in diagnostic grouping of subjects, in the settings where research is carried out, in ages of group members and size of group.

Social skills curriculum

Most social skills curriculums cover the broad social skill areas used within the approach addressed in this book. However, it is the importance of teaching social skills within the framework of understanding social competencies (i.e., understanding key variables and core deficits), peer-based group approaches, and stages of group development, that is emphasized here. Figure 5.1 provides a general list of social skills frequently addressed, while Appendices 4.1–4.5 list social skills as they relate to the specific stages of development to be discussed in Chapter 14.

PART III

GROUP INTERVENTIONS WITH CHILDREN WITH AUTISM SPECTRUM DISORDERS

Part III describes the specific group model which was developed to make use of and combine group therapy principles, a process-oriented approach, structured cognitive-behavioral techniques, and skill-based instruction. Within the group setting, a unique opportunity is provided to create an environment where the focus is on both the individual within the group and the group as a whole. Within this group structure, this approach follows a cognitive-developmental model that tracks and builds upon the individual's development through stages within the group. This approach builds systematically an understanding of the individual's own capacities and abilities to engage others as well as their areas of difficulties and weakness, then uses this information to develop a plan to address these issues and concerns in a developmentally sequenced manner.

First, the model employed here is described in detail, with emphasis on its group therapy underpinnings, on the rationale for group-focused and peer-based interventions with ASD individuals, and on the specific types of group interventions chosen for use within the model here. Next is a description of how data and information are collected on potential group members to define areas of interest and to construct individual goals. Once a set of individual goals is constructed and the individual is placed within a group, then this information is integrated with information of other group members in the formulation of group goals.

Stages of group development are then described and defined within this context. As the group proceeds through the stages of group development and as the group members focus on individual and group goal attainment, group participants are then taught the necessary and relevant skills to effectively and in age appropriate ways interact with peers in the natural group setting. In this context, the group's strengths and relationship capacities are engaged to enable and facilitate the necessary skill building that follows.

Chapter 11

A Model for Group Interventions for Children with ASD

Although questions have been raised about the usefulness of traditional therapeutic approaches with individuals with Autism Spectrum Disorder (ASD) (Attwood 2007; Jacobsen 2003), group therapeutic approaches, while requiring some adaptation and modification, in many ways appear as the most appropriate and well-suited interventions to address the personal and interpersonal needs of ASD individuals. Clearly, there are many issues presented by these children, such as those of anxiety and stress management, joint attention, and flexibility, change, and transition mentioned previously, that will influence and affect the ability of the ASD individual to effectively use therapeutic interventions. However, it does appear possible that by recognizing their impact and by putting structures in place to address and overcome these issues, that the ASD individual can benefit from psychotherapeutically-based approaches, particularly group-focused, peer-based interventions. While individual and group psychotherapy should only be conducted by appropriately trained and credentialed professionals, psychotherapeutic process and psychotherapeutic approaches have much to offer in understanding how to consider and to address the issues that ASD individuals present, particularly within the group setting.

The application of psychotherapeutic approaches in a group setting with children with ASD

Psychotherapy is a communication process. It is a process where an individual learns how to share and explore problems with another individual, a therapist, and together they work toward solutions. Whether the problems are related to thoughts, feelings, behaviors, interactions, or combinations of these, possible solutions to the problems which occur are considered, discussed, practiced, tried out, often modified, and tried again in a push to improve the world of the individual. This is the therapeutic process.

Psychotherapy with ASD individuals is also a communication process. However, it also differs from the traditional psychotherapy process with a non-ASD individual because the ASD individual has difficulty with the communication process itself and must often learn first "how" to communicate, how to express oneself accurately and appropriately, and how to read and understand the communications of others, again accurately and appropriately. Psychotherapy for the ASD individual is about learning how and what to communicate, how and why to express and articulate problems, and how best to solve these problems with the strengths and limitations that the individual themselves possesses. This is the therapeutic process for the ASD individual.

Psychotherapy is a process of self-awareness and of interaction, where the individual learns about specific aspects of themselves, including their own individual needs, and then must decide when and how to modify certain aspects of themselves to address these needs. The individual must learn to take ownership for their own personal feelings, behaviors, or interactions. For example, they must learn not just what triggers their sadness or anger, but why these feelings or behaviors occur, what effects they have on themselves and on others, and most importantly, what they can choose to do about them.

Psychotherapy with the ASD individual is also a process of self-awareness, of learning about one's own unique issues and concerns, how they are related to ASD, and how they may affect one's interactions with the world around them. It is this process of self-awareness that leads the ASD individual to understand their disorder and its effects, to learn how to express these issues accurately and appropriately to others, and to take ownership and responsibility for their own thoughts, behaviors, and actions, whether related to ASD or not.

Psychotherapy is an interaction process. Most basically, it occurs between an individual and a therapist in a process of communication, exploration, and self-awareness. Psychotherapy with the ASD individual is also an interaction process, but in addition to exploring the process of interaction between the individual and therapist, it also must address and explore the unique problems that will arise in interactions and communications resulting from the ASD itself. Given the problems inherent in ASD, the therapist must join with the ASD individual in understanding the individual's problems and concerns, in how they relate to the issues of ASD, and in seeking solutions that best fit the individual and their needs.

Psychotherapy can also occur as a set of interactions between a therapist and several individuals in a group. While many of the same principles of psychotherapy apply in both individual and group situations, the focus here is on those principles that relate specifically to group psychotherapeutic processes as applicable with individuals with ASD. As such, modifications of these processes for use with ASD individuals must be considered and tailored to the needs of these individuals.

Underlying therapeutic principles guiding group interventions with all individuals

In a classic work on psychotherapy (Haworth 1964), Axline outlined the basic principles necessary for effective psychotherapy with children which are adapted here to apply to group interventions with ASD children. These form the basis for the approach described in this book. They include:

1. The group leader as therapist develops a warm empathic relationship with each group member.

2. The group leader recognizes and encourages each group member's right to express themselves through thoughts, feelings, emotions, and appropriate behaviors.

3. The group leader and group participants understand and explicitly agree to engage and interact with one another on the basis of honesty and respect.

4. The group setting and environment will be a safe, supportive, open environment where thoughts, feelings, and emotions can be shared in an open, honest, and respectful way between group participants without concern for one's physical or emotional safety.

5. Each group participant is expected to take ownership and responsibility for their own statements and behaviors and to attempt to understand how these are understood and interpreted by other group participants.

6. The primary rule in group therapy relates to *respect* – respect for the group leader, respect for oneself, respect for others in the group, respect for things that are brought into or used in the group, respect for one's own and other's thoughts, feelings, and emotions.

7. The group leader maintains responsibility for creating and maintaining the group structure, including setting, clarifying, and enforcing rules, boundaries, and limits when necessary.

8. A group structure is established, agreed upon, and adhered to by all group participants.

Within the group approach discussed here, consistent emphasis throughout is placed on the structure and progression within the group as it relates specifically to:

- the recognition of and adherence to the need for respect in all facets of interaction within the group

- the need to build and maintain rapport and cohesion within the group

- the need for rules and limits and an understanding of what is allowed and what is not allowed

- the importance of and focus on relationships and connections established, fostered, and maintained within the group

- a willingness to recognize, process, and understand what happens within the group, such as
  - attending to issues of anxiety, attention, and flexibility
  - learning skills necessary to make relationships work.

The rationale for group interventions with ASD individuals

ASD involves an impairment of social interaction and social communication. Individuals with ASD typically demonstrate significant problems in multiple areas of social functioning and while there may be variation from individual to individual in how this manifests itself, impairments in social-interpersonal functioning are core deficits. Therefore, it is important to understand the strengths and limitations of the ASD individual and how these affect and influence social interpersonal interactions. In this context, it is also believed that the learning and development of appropriate social-interactive skills is best achieved within a group environment that is sensitive to the issues, concerns, and needs of both individuals within the group and of the group itself.

Individuals with ASD are described by a range of difficulties and problems relating to social interactions. They may appear aloof, disconnected, and ignore others, they may be unaware of physical boundaries and invade the space of others, they may be annoying, confrontative, even aggressive, with others. The list of potential social interactive difficulties and problems for the ASD individual is long. From the ASD individual's perspective, they may feel misunderstood, constantly criticized, isolated, alienated, ignored and left out of group activities, scapegoated and targeted, and frequently frustrated and discouraged. They are reported to experience more social isolation and loneliness (Bauminger, Shulman, and Agam 2003), higher sensitivity to criticism (Wing 1981), and a greater risk for dysthymia and depression (Ghaziuddin, Ghaziuddin, and Greden 2002; Szatmari 1991).

Group situations can bring members together who share similar interests, function at similar levels of social and emotional development, and have similar needs for the understanding of social interactions and the learning of necessary social skills. Group interventions provide members with opportunities to experience and discuss issues related to personal struggles and concerns (i.e., my feelings, my thoughts, etc.), related to general interpersonal issues (i.e., interactions at school, at home, etc.), and related to interpersonal issues which might arise within the group (i.e., with group members, between group members). Within the group structure, members are able to relate to the unique culture established for that group, to connect with peers around common issues and concerns, and to use these connections and the culture as a force for change, growth, and development.

Group interventions provide the participants with opportunities to address issues related to behavior, feelings, and thinking which can be enhanced through the use of:

- homogeneous grouping
- individual and group goal setting
- ongoing and consistent peer connections
- therapeutic interactions.

Homogeneous grouping

Homogeneous grouping, that is, grouping that is based on common factors and variables shared by all members of a group, forms the basis for the group structure described in this book. With the groups described here using homogenous grouping, a combination of age and developmental level serves as the first criteria. Groups are constructed having a two-year age span (e.g., 6–7 years, 7–8 years, 8–9 years, etc.). This allows for placement of a developmentally "more mature" seven-year-old in a 7–8 year old group where issues will more accurately reflect his/her developmental level, and a developmentally "less mature" seven-year-old in a 6–7 year old group for the same reasons.

Also, during the application process, all group members are evaluated on the Initial Evaluation and Interview Form (Figure 12.2, described in Chapter 12) for the presence or absence of several individual, personal and interpersonal variables considered important for social interaction. As described in previous chapters, these variables include the three key issues (often referred to as "core deficits") with ASD individuals of anxiety (its experience, expression, control, and management), attention (individual capacities for focused, sustained, selective, flexible, and joint forms), and flexibility, change, and transition (its speed and efficiency). Other variables assessed include: self-control/self-management, the ability to manage and control physical and emotional impulses as they arise in increasingly stimulating environments; sensory issues, the general levels of tolerable stimulation including the internal and external environmental needs of the individual (sound/noise levels, physical space issues, visual inputs); general social interpersonal capacities, a range of skills used to interact with another individual on verbal, physical, emotional, and behavioral levels; relatedness, the capacity to find a way to connect interpersonally and emotionally with another individual who is physically present at that moment; theory of mind, the capacity to take or understand another individual's point of view, way of thinking, or position on an issue or topic; and peer relationships, the demonstration in the real world (i.e., school, neighborhood, afterschool activities) of the ability to establish, maintain, and nurture extended and meaningful relationships and friendships.

With a general understanding of the ASD individual's functioning on these nine variables, a general profile of group proficiency (abilities and skills) is established. This profile is then used as the primary tool for understanding how the individual may function in a group situation, with consideration given to how this particular ASD individual will "match" with other ASD individuals. On this basis, group members are selected based on their ability to "match" with others on similar variables.

Homogeneous grouping, by age, developmental level, and personal/interpersonal characteristics, allows for the structuring of process and skill-based tasks and activities that are geared for particular stages of group development (described in Chapter 14). For example, homogenous grouping allows group members to more quickly identify with each other and the group, based on common, shared variables, to establish a common group culture on which the group process may develop, and to acknowledge common shared deficits and their effects (Brown, Hedlinger, and Mieling 1995).

Individual and group goal setting

Group interventions provide opportunities for individuals to join with others in working on common shared issues and concerns through individual and group goal setting. This process is believed to be twofold in that it includes first the establishment of individual goals for each member, and then, as the group forms and develops, the creation of group goals by all participants as they join in a common focus and recognize a common set of needs.

The initial step in this goal setting process is for each member to understand why they are in the group and what they are there to work on. This begins in the initial interview with each individual and family where there is a discussion of parent issues and concerns, teacher data on school based issues and concerns, information from checklists, and the individual's own expressed interests and concerns. This results in the creation of a list of "areas of interests" for the individual which provides a preliminary understanding of each individual's capacities to function with others in a group situation and of the ways in which individuals would "match" in a group situation with other similar individuals. This forms the basis for member selection determined by age, developmental level, personal/interpersonal characteristics, and "areas of interest."

Each individual's "areas of interest" form the basis for the creation of individual goals that will be focused on within the group (see Chapter 12, Figure 12.3). These "areas of interest" and individual goals are discussed and clarified with the ASD individual and their parents/caretakers with the understanding that these are issues that may be addressed in the group. Each participant then enters the group with a basic understanding of their own "areas of interest," of their own individual goals, and of the importance of the goal setting process. Following the construction and initiation of a group with several participants similar in age, developmental level, and social-emotional functioning, and with similar and consistent individual goals, group members get to know one another during this initial stage, share personal information, observe how each other functions in a group situation, and experience how peers react to them. At this point, each group member must recognize and understand that they will be part of a group and must join with other participants in the establishment and setting of group goals, that is, goals that apply to the ongoing development of the group as a whole. As this process unfolds, group goals can be addressed and focused on.

Setting group goals requires that participants begin the process of orienting to one another and to the group as a whole and of learning about group interaction and group decision-making. Typically, groups are constructed of ASD individuals who have similar individual goals to be worked on at the outset of the group experience. The individual goals for each group member are then used to construct group goals for that particular group. Initially, groups typically create group goals similar to their individual goals but, relatively quickly, they recognize the differences between individual and group goals and join together led by the group leader in the establishing of group goals based on shared intersections of interests, needs, issues, and concerns. The group goals are constructed based on the specific stage of group development that the group is at (as described in Chapter 14). For example, each group beginning at a Stage 1 level of Group Formation and

Orientation will have constructed specific group goals relating to this stage. For example, Stage 1 group goals may be, "The group will learn what each member's favorite hobby (food, TV show, etc.) is." As the group moves through a particular stage and the next stage is approached, group leaders review individual goals of all participants, then, in discussion with the group, modify group goals or construct new goals as needed. It is this process of shared discussion and interaction on how to create group goals and what they will address that signals forward progress through the initial stage of Group Formation and Orientation and toward the second stage of Group Cohesion.

While groups proceed at different rates and function at different levels, it is necessary for the group leader to be active in encouraging and fostering the establishment and modification of ongoing group goals. At the same time, the group leader must be patient as the group initially relies on their own individual goals to get themselves going before getting to the point of being ready and able to join together in the creation of group goals. Throughout however, the group leader is aware of each participant's "areas of interest" and individual goals so that the group leader may steer and direct the formation of the group goals in keeping with the developmental, cognitive, behavioral, emotional, and social needs of the group. Examples of Individual and Group Goals are provided in Appendices 2 and 3.

Peer connections

The group format is employed and emphasized in this approach with ASD individuals because it provides a safe haven for group members to establish connections at their own pace to each individual group member and to the group as a whole. With opportunities for in depth individual and group peer connections, each member can learn about social interactions, how to take social-interpersonal risks, how to express and experience both positive and negative affects and emotions in group situations, and what it is like to be accepted and understood by peers. Within the group, individual members are able to address stress and anxiety-related issues as they arise within each stage of group development and as the result of various group interactions. New and previously experienced stress and anxiety producing situations that are related to individual interpersonal interactions and to specific situational or environmental triggers can also be addressed.

In the group situation, members may also address how variable attentional capacities (focused, sustained, selective, flexible, joint) affect and influence peer connections and interactions and how best to manage these situations. Group members are also provided real-life opportunities to address issues of flexibility, change, and transition, as they arise in the moment to moment life of the group. Over time, internal comfort and security are established within the group, allowing members to experience and to express emotions, to receive honest and constructive feedback, and to learn and to employ new strategies and techniques to manage and cope more effectively in the social domain.

Therapeutic interactions

The group setting provides ongoing and frequent opportunities for the group leader to use existing situations and to create new situations which allow therapeutic interchanges to be experienced both directly and indirectly by all group members. The therapeutic value of the group experience for ASD individuals exists within the interactions themselves, in learning how to communicate with others more effectively, in gaining increased self-awareness, and through repeated interpersonal interactions and experiences. From there, new responses can be constructed (Mishna and Muskat 1998).

Therapeutic interactions in this context occur between the group leader and individuals, between the group leader and the group as a whole, between an individual group member and another individual group member, and between individual group members and the group as a whole. Therapeutic interactions are always embedded within a relationship, emphasizing the relatedness and connectedness that occurs between individuals separately or as a group. They are respectful and accepting of the individual as a person or as part of a group and as existing with a range of thoughts, feelings, and impulses, many of which seek expression. Therapeutic interactions are genuine and convey honest communication in a safe and supportive manner. It is in this context that the underlying therapeutic principles guiding group interventions, described earlier in this chapter, are applied.

Types of group intervention approaches

While the underlying rationale for using group approaches to address the social impairments of ASD individuals is based upon the importance of homogeneous grouping, individual and group goal setting, peer connections, and therapeutic interactions, several different types of interventions were selected for use within this approach to enhance the benefits of grouping, goal setting, peer interactions, and therapeutic interactions. While these types of group approaches differ in significant ways, they also overlap in many other ways and appear best suited to emphasize the key concepts of this approach to group situations with ASD individuals. These include the use of:

1.   small group format
2.   developmental leveling

3. self-management
4. peer-mediated approach
5. priming
6. pivotal response training
7. direct instruction
8. written scripts.

1. *Small group format*

The small group format employed in this approach typically consists of four or five ASD individuals with one group leader or five or six ASD individuals with two group leaders. Since group members are also selected on the basis of similar "areas of interest" and individual group goals, the likelihood of strong and positive connections is increased. Keeping group membership at low and manageable levels is intended to purposely encourage and create more relationship opportunities between group participants early in the group experience and to foster more intense interactions and connections later in the group experience.

The small group format also allows for the construction and maintenance of a group structure that meets the needs and individual goals of each group member. In the beginning, this will include setting up a structure to encourage and foster interaction, later a structure that will require addressing and managing conflict and confrontation and, still later, a structure that will include understanding, processing, and integrating interactional information. With a small, limited number of group participants, it is possible to focus specifically on an individual's areas of interest and individual goals and gradually join these with the group goals constructed for the particular stage of group development. The small group format also makes possible the construction of more specific and directed group goals as well as allowing the broader group goals to more quickly and readily shift based on the group's development as it moves through different stages of group evolution.

For example, it is believed that a smaller group size more quickly and more smoothly fosters the initial group adjustment and orientation to the group process and hastens the connections and cohesion that develops between group members. With fewer participants, members are more likely to foster connections of greater intensity between one another, all of which can be closely monitored, directed, and redirected as needed by the group leader.

The small group format also assures a close connection between group members and the group leader, utilizing a constant feedback loop of what works and what doesn't as the group leader initiates and facilitates appropriate task and activity selection consistent with the current stage of group development. It also allows each individual member to be more involved directly in task and activity construction and selection, forces members to discuss issues and work together, and requires the addressing and resolution of differences and conflicts. Working in smaller groups allows the group leader to use the developing group cohesion, peer connections, and interactive intensity in therapeutically useful and beneficial ways, to stay attuned to the variety of interactive experiences, and to respond to situations in timely and informed ways.

2. *Developmental leveling*

As part of the comprehensive intake and interview process, information from a variety of sources is collected and used to make informed decisions about group placement. Information from past and current evaluations, parent and teacher observations, and interview data, provide the basis for understanding an individual's cognitive, behavioral, learning, and emotional styles. Reviewing evaluation data is particularly helpful in establishing an understanding of an individual's general developmental level in these areas. Individuals with similar levels of cognitive development may share similar interests in this area, while individuals at similar levels of behavioral development may require similar levels of external structure. Individuals with similar levels of emotional development may benefit from certain types of support and feedback, while individuals with similar levels of learning and skill development may share educational interests.

The approach emphasized here also requires an understanding of the developmental level in key areas for each group member as well as the overall developmental level of the group as a whole. At the outset of the group, the group leader relies heavily on the information collected from parents and teachers prior to beginning group. This provides both a general and specific understanding of the individual's learning, cognitive, and social-emotional style and what to anticipate as the group members begin to address individual and group goals. This information also provides an understanding of the individual's profile of strengths and limitations and how these can be accessed to encourage growth fostering, developmentally and age appropriate experiences. This data is also used for grouping potential group participants. While homogeneous grouping, based on group members' overall similarities, provides a basis for forming the group, an understanding of both the individual's and the group's developmental level provides the basis for establishing individual and group goals and for the development of specific task and activities, particularly when directed toward developing and increasing the frequency and quality of social interactions.

As groups proceed, increasing emphasis is placed on group leader observations of specific tasks and activities and interventions that succeed, group members' feedback to one another, and constant monitoring of the session to session performance by the group on the specific tasks and activities selected for each group goal. Group goals and activities are adjusted and modified frequently to stay in line with the overall developmental level of both individuals and the group.

3. *Self-management*

In this approach, heavy emphasis is placed on self-management and self-control by each individual group member with the goal of developing strategies to understand, manage, and control their own behavior, thoughts, and emotions. Discussions are initiated by the group leader about how self-management requires an understanding of oneself and one's typical responses to different situations, how it requires an understanding of the nature of social situations, and how it requires an understanding of what responses are required in which situation. The expectation and requirement for self-management and self-control in social situations is connected to the need for effective management of varying degrees and states of stress and anxiety related to both individual and group social situations, to needs for close and directed attention, and to needs for flexibility and change depending on the situation. As such, self management and self control in social situations are understood as the most important and often the most difficult facets of social competence for ASD individuals.

Emphasis here is on a model requiring group members to take increasing responsibility for understanding, managing and controlling, and directing their own personal and interpersonal communications and interactions with others. From the outset of group, both individual and group goals focus on increasing personal and interpersonal self-management and self-control through training, practice, and reinforcement. Group members are expected to take increasing ownership and responsibility of this process and to learn strategies that can be applied consistently and effectively in natural group settings. This includes learning and practicing how to self-monitor and self-reinforce with both tangible and intangible reinforcers.

4. *Peer-mediated approach*

The group-based approach described here employs a structured peer mediated approach utilizing the extensive research and positive results of this approach with instructional groups. Peer-mediated approaches emphasize the power and importance of peer to peer interactions when peers are placed in active, instructional roles, learning and teaching one another skills for effective advancement. This approach places emphasis on structure, direction, self-awareness and self-management, systematic skill building, consistent monitoring, and frequent feedback within a sequential and progressive model that places increasing responsibility on the group members themselves to move their group forward.

Within the small group setting, with group members placed based on similar developmental levels, and with an emphasis on self-management and self-control, the group leader gradually places increasing expectations on group members to be aware of their own individual and group goals, to take an active role in meeting then reconstructing their individual and group goals, and to learn how to participate in taking control and running their group so as to achieve these mutual, reciprocal goals.

The small group format with significant leader involvement allows group members to gradually assume roles of increasing self and group responsibility and to actively and cooperatively work with other group members in moving the group forward. This approach emphasizes setting and holding to a clear structure and set of expectations, significant practice and orientation to all tasks and activities provided, including a discussion and understanding of the rationale and purpose of their use, clear instructions and skill building in ways to succeed, close monitoring of performance and progress with adjustments and modifications as necessary, and constant and consistent feedback to group members.

5.   *Priming*

In this approach, the concept of priming is used to introduce new information and new skills, to reduce and manage related anxiety and stress, and to provide a consistent and predictable approach. Priming involves preparing the group members for the introduction of new information, a new task or activity, or a new way of approaching and managing a problematic situation. This is done by breaking complex tasks into simple steps, then preparing and training the group to manage the initial parts of the new information with previously learned skills and strategies. Following this, subsequent steps are introduced and merged with previously learned steps, until the task is completely learned.

Group members are prepared in advance to anticipate and respond to the new information to be presented and are desensitized to any stress or anxiety related to the upcoming information by the use and practice of stress and anxiety control and management techniques. They are encouraged to rely on learned strategies and techniques and skills that have been successful and reinforcing as they develop and consider new strategies and skills. When presenting new information, initial steps in the task are introduced in low stress situations, with reduced cognitive, behavioral, and social demands. Initial successes are heavily reinforced, then gradually followed with subsequent steps, reinforced and supported as needed and with stress and anxiety management techniques as indicated. As new tasks are moved into, additional strategies are taught and employed to address the new information or situations and attempts are made to integrate any new information and skills with previously learned skills. This process is repeated with each new task and each new step in the learning process, constantly making use of previously employed strategies and techniques to learn and master the new information and tasks.

6. *Pivotal Response Training (PRT)*

Principles of Pivotal Response Training (PRT) are used and adapted for ASD individuals to fit with other aspects of this peer-based, group-focused, skill-directed intervention approach. PRT, an intervention that primarily employs applied behavioral techniques, focuses on training in pivotal areas, such as behavior, language, and social interaction, through the use of motivation, multiple cues, and self-management (Koegel and Frea 1993). The focus here is on learning and increasing the frequency of social interaction while managing behaviors that could interfere with this process.

The small group, peer-based approach described here focuses on and encourages group member initiation and agreement on tasks and activities, group member direction of tasks and activities when appropriate, and mutual reinforcement of success and appropriate behaviors, as motivating influences. The group leader facilitates a task and activity selection process that begins with less demanding, more manageable tasks with a higher likelihood for success and gradually moves toward more demanding, challenging, and anxiety-arousing tasks and activities. Group members are provided with strategies and techniques to manage stress and anxiety as it arises related to both the tasks and activities and the group and individual interaction process, with self-motivating and peer-motivating affirmation statements and techniques, and with learned positive optimism approaches.

Other PRT components emphasized throughout this goal-based approach are active choice, clear instructions, consistent reinforcement, and multiple presentations in slightly different form of the same skill. Throughout this process, principles of PRT are merged with priming concepts. PRT provides the group leader with techniques to understand, target, and respond to important areas of social interaction and related behaviors, while priming concepts encourage the group leader to move sequentially and systematically through the steps of teaching specific social skills. PRT and priming both allow the "spiraling effect" to take hold and influence the recognition and learning of process variables (stress/anxiety management, joint attention, flexibility/transitions, etc.) and the learning of specific social skills (initiating conversation, asking questions, providing feedback, etc.). There is some research support that with consistent effort these components support generalization across setting and activities (Pierce and Schreibman 1995, 1997).

7. *Direct instruction*

Based on information collected, observations, and the construction of individual and group goals, the group leader selects specific skills to be taught based on this accumulated information. This approach assumes that group members possess a wide range of interactive skills, but also with significant and varied areas of deficit. Attempts are made to use and build on areas of strength to target these deficit areas and to specify the necessary skills to be taught, practiced, reinforced, and generalized, employing principles of priming and PRT. Specific skills to be taught are selected by the group leader based on areas of interest and individual and group goals. The group leader then breaks down complex social skills into simple steps that can be learned, practiced, and reinforced within each weekly group as well as over time. The specific skills presented are intended to fit each of the group member's cognitive, language/communication, and social-emotional capacities.

As the groups proceed, members are encouraged to interact with one another about their experiences and strategies in skill learning, to help their peers understand and manage points or areas of difficulty, and to work together in developing strategies to succeed and move forward. Within this approach, group members learn how to understand and work with both their strengths and limitations in group interaction and to take increasing responsibility for their group behavior and social-interpersonal interactions.

8. *Written scripts*

The development of written scripts as a specific type of intervention (Charlop-Christy and Kelso 2003; Volden and Johnston 1999) has been used to focus on and teach specific skills and appropriate behavior as it relates to specific events and situations. These events and situations can be initiated by adults working with ASD individuals or can be taken from the ASD individual's own daily interactions. Written scripts are then constructed either by an adult or together with the ASD individual that include characters, themes, certain environments and situations, a range of possible social behaviors, outcomes, and feedback. Written scripts provide opportunities for ASD individuals to address specific issues and concerns that may be encountered or in many instances, situations that may be of ongoing concern (i.e., teasing, bullying, approaching unfamiliar situations, etc.).

The use of Social Stories is a specific intervention developed by Gray (1998, 2000) and addresses what is happening, who is involved, where is it occurring, why is it happening, when the situation is taking place, and what the most age appropriate responses or outcomes for the specific situation may be. Social Stories employ the use of written scripts, direct instruction, self-management, developmental leveling, priming, and managing and regulating affective reaction and responses, and have been demonstrated to be most effective when used in combination with other types of interventions (Scattone, Tingstrom, and Wilczynski 2006).

Chapter 12

Forming an Understanding of the ASD Individual

Overview

In this approach, emphasis is placed on establishing a comprehensive understanding of the individual with Autism Spectrum Disorder (ASD)'s current needs and areas of concern, particularly as these needs relate to the presence or absence of social competencies and social skills. To accomplish this, relevant information is extracted from collected history and previous evaluations, past and present intervention reports, and current parent and teacher observational data. This includes information related to diagnostic considerations and questions and the ASD individual's patterns of existing strengths and limitations. When these sets of information and observations have been acquired, specific questions can then be generated for face to face interviews. Ultimately, this information will be used to determine areas of interest and to construct individual goals for each individual, and finally, group goals when the individual is placed within a group.

Collecting information relevant to group interventions

Referrals to the type of program described here will typically come from a variety of sources. These include medical and mental health professionals working in related fields, educators and school professionals, individuals in related professional organizations, and parents and individuals familiar with the program. Typically, an initial direct contact occurs to discuss the appropriateness of the program for the ASD individual. Following this, if appropriate, extensive and relevant background medical, developmental, educational, and mental health histories are requested, with a particular focus on social interactions and social skill development.

This process requires that parents/caretakers of the ASD individual provide documents, medical records, previous assessments and evaluations, pertinent school records, and information regarding previous interventions. A face to face interview is also required of both parent/caretaker and ASD individual with at least part of the time being a joint interview of the parent/caretaker and ASD individual together in interaction. These interviews include a complete developmental and family history. At this point, arrangements are also made for the collection of teacher observations as well as those of any other professionals or para-professionals working with the ASD individual.

Next, but prior to beginning group, parents and teachers are required to complete several formal and informal checklists that address social competence and social interactions in both group and individual home and school settings. These checklists were created or selected specifically to assess the particular needs of the ASD individuals and to guide the construction of appropriate goals within the social interactive group setting. Some checklists are formal, standardized procedures while others are informal program-specific measures. They are used to assess and measure functioning in various situations and at different points in time and to compare the functioning of these individuals to both typical and nontypical standardized populations. The checklists collect information relating to the individual's ability to function within group situations as rated by adult observers who know the individual well. These checklists and procedures may also be used to assess an individual's progress over time regarding the group interventions provided when administered at different points in the group process (e.g., beginning, middle, and end of an individual's group participation).

The intent of gathering such extensive information is multifaceted. The primary intent is to assess and understand the ASD individual's social competence and social skill development in order to construct an appropriate plan of action for moving forward. Given the nature of ASD as a significant impairment in social interaction with related problems in understanding and engaging in age appropriate peer relationships, the requested information is a necessary component in addressing the ASD individual's issues in social relationships in a systematic way, fully informed by all available diagnostic and treatment information. Following interview, data collection, and review of this necessary information, decisions about appropriate behavioral and treatment interventions are then considered. Given the range of interventions available and the demonstrated deficits in social interaction that ASD individuals experience, peer-based group experiences within a therapeutically-based and skill-focused, cognitive-developmental model appear as an extremely beneficial and effective intervention, particularly when combined with other interventions.

All the information collected is reviewed by the group leader prior to the start of the group and forms the basis for constructing areas of interest for each child. Areas of interest are defined as issues of concern designated by both parents and teachers, that is, concerning or problematic behaviors or interactions noted both at home and at school by adult observers in situations prior to beginning in the group. Examples of areas of interest selected may be broad, such as, "tries to control discussions," to the more specific, such as, "refuses to share personal information." Additionally, the data collected provide information regarding appropriate group placement as well as to informing the process of individual and group goal development.

In working with ASD individuals, the following forms have been developed to aid in the understanding of the social competencies and social skill development of the ASD individual and to guide decisions about acceptance for a group experience, placement in a specific social competency group, and construction of appropriate individual and group goals.

Test Information and Data Sheet (Figure 12.1)

This form collects in one place information considered relevant to the approach employed here and is completed as soon as all past and current evaluations, reports, and communications have been received. This form includes test data and information about learning, cognitive, and social-emotional styles as demonstrated on previous evaluations completed. An attempt is made to understand the ASD individual's cognitive abilities and style, language and communication patterns, neurocognitive capacities (i.e., visual-spatial, attentional, memory, organizational capacities), academic skill development, and social-emotional functioning. Emphasis is placed on understanding both the presence and development of underlying structures and the attainment and precision of specific skills. This information is generally obtained from parents and other professionals working with the ASD individual prior to the initial interview and provides a general sense of the ASD individual's overall profile of strengths and limitations as well as allowing for the construction of specific questions for the face to face interviews.

✓

Figure 12.1 Social Competency and Social Skills Groups

Test Information and Data Sheet

Name: Grade:

Date of birth: School:

Age: City/Town:

Dates of testing:

Diagnoses (include all
given and dates):

Cognitive functioning:

Wechsler (or Stanford-Binet, Kaufman, Woodcock-Johnson, etc.) scores

Verbal score	Index scores	Subtest scores
Performance score		
Full scale		
Verbal-Performance difference		

Overall level of cognitive functioning

Language processing   Receptive

                           Expressive

                           Other communication
                           issues

Overall level of language processing and functioning:

Visual-perceptual-Spatial-Motor functioning

• Motor

• Visual perceptual

• Visual motor

• Visual Motor Perceptual Integrative

Overall level of Visual-Perceptual-Spatial-Motor functioning

Attention   • Visual

             • Auditory

Memory   • Visual

             • Auditory

Executive functioning	Inhibition/Delay	Mental shifting	Initiation
	Idea generation	Planning	Organization
	Working memory	Decision making	
	Problem solving	Self-monitoring/Self-checking	

Social-Emotional	Depression	Self-concept/ Sense of self
	Anxiety	Understanding of emotions
	Quality of thinking	

Academic skill development:

	Reading:	• Recognition	• Comprehension
	Mathematics:	• Computation	• Concepts
	Written expression:	• Spelling	• Writing

Summary:
• Learning style:
• Cognitive style:
• Social-emotional style:

Strengths:

Weaknesses:

Specific questions for face to face interviews:

• Parents:

• ASD individual:

Other relevant information:

Clinician name: Date:

Figure 12.2 Social Competency and Social Skills Group

Initial Evaluation and Interview Form

Name: Grade:

Date of birth: School:

Age: City/Town:

Interview attendees: Date of interview:

Diagnoses (provide all given with dates):

Relevant history (Family, Developmental, Medical, Academic):

Appearance/presentation of ASD individual:

Issues profile (Provide relevant examples; rate 1–5 (low–high)):

Attention (focused, sustained, selective, flexible, joint):

Sensory issues (tactile, visual, auditory, taste, olfactory, body perception):

Relatedness (emotional connections, physical connections):

Social interpersonal capacities (verbal, physical, emotional, behavioral):

Self-control/Self-management (self-awareness, self-insight, impulse control):

Stress and anxiety control and management (strategies):

Flexibility/ability to change and transition (obsessive-compulsive habits):

Theory of mind (awareness of others, sensitivity to others, sympathy, empathy):

Peer relationships/friendships (none, one, two, or three friends; isolated play/behavior; parallel play/behavior; interactive play (not effective, mildly effective, moderately effective, very effective):

Appropriateness for group (Rate 1–5 (low–high)):

Clinician name: Date:

Initial Evaluation and Interview Form (Figure 12.2)

This form is completed during or shortly after the face to face interview with the parent/caretaker and ASD individual. It includes observational data that is considered important for group placement decisions and to help understand the ASD individual's "areas of interest," that is, those issues or concerns to be addressed within the group.

The Initial Evaluation and Interview Form focuses primarily on specific personal and interpersonal issues which appear to be of critical importance for the ASD individual and necessary for social interchange. Nine specific issues are addressed on the form and relevant examples of each are recorded when observed in the interview, particularly those areas known to be deficient in ASD individuals (often referred to as "core deficits"). Each is rated on a scale from 1–5 (low-high). Also, observations, collected information, and examples of several other key concepts important for an understanding of the ASD individual are obtained and noted on this form with a final global statement about the ASD individual's appropriateness for placement in a group.

Individual Profile – Stress-Anxiety Assessment (Figure 6.2)

The Stress-Anxiety Assessment (also discussed in Chapter 6) is a checklist containing twelve items that parents/caretakers are requested to complete at or shortly following the initial intake interview. The twelve items provide the group leader with specific information about how the ASD individual manages and copes with different stress-anxiety-related issues. Each item is rated on a scale from 1–5, ranging from never (a score of 1) to always (a score of 5). The total of these twelve ratings is summed and a Total Anxiety Score is obtained. A general Anxiety Assessment Scoring Continuum is included at the end of the assessment to provide a general guide to the group leader as to where the individual will fall on the continuum which ranges from High stress/Anxiety and Low coping/Management (a score of 12) to Manages stress/Anxiety and Good coping/Management (a score of 60).

This information from the Stress-Anxiety Assessment and the ratings given provide the group leader with additional data with which to understand areas of interests and to develop individual and group goals.

Individual Profile – Attention Assessment (Figure 7.7)

The Attention Assessment (also discussed in Chapter 7) is a checklist containing twenty items that parents/caretakers are requested to complete at or shortly following the initial intake interview. The twenty items are divided into five sections, each relating to a specific area of attention and each consisting of four items. These five areas of attention follow the developmental progression of attention described in Chapter 7. The four items within each area provide the group leader with specific information about how the ASD individual functions in that specific area of attention. Each item is rated on a scale from 1–5, ranging from never (a score of 1) to always (a score of 5). The total of the four ratings within each area is summed and an Attention Score for each area is obtained. The total sum of the 20 items provides a Total Attention Score. A general Attention Assessment Scoring Continuum is included at the end of the assessment to provide a general guide to the group leader as to where the individual will fall on the continuum for both the specific attention areas and for the total score. This ranges from Low Attention (a score of 4 for the specific areas, a score of 20 for the total score) to High Attention (a score of 20 for the specific areas, a score of 100 for the total score).

This information from the Attention Assessment and the ratings given provide the group leader with additional data with which to understand areas of interests and to develop individual and group goals.

Individual Profile – Flexibility, Change and Transition Assessment (Figure 8.2)

The Flexibility, Change, and Transition Assessment (also discussed in Chapter 8) is a checklist containing five items that parents/caretakers are requested to complete at or shortly following the initial intake interview. The five items provide the group leader with specific information about how the ASD individual deals with issues and situations requiring flexibility, change, and transition. Each item is rated on a scale from 1–5, ranging from never (a score of 1) to always (a score of 5). The total of these five ratings is summed and a Total Flexibility, Change, and Transition Score is obtained. A general Flexibility, Change, and Transition Assessment Scoring Continuum is included at the end of the assessment to provide a general guide to the group leader as to where the individual will fall on the continuum which ranges from High inflexibility, low capacity for change or transition (a score of 5) to High flexibility, good capacity for change and transition (a score of 25).

This information from the Flexibility, Change, and Transition Assessment and the ratings given provide the group leader with additional data with which to understand areas of interest and to develop individual and group goals.

Areas of Interest Form (Figure 12.3)

This form is used to compile "areas of interest" collected from parents/caretakers, teachers, other professionals, interviewers of the ASD individual, and when appropriate, the ASD individual him/herself. This information is gathered from previous reports and evaluations provided, telephone consultations, interview information, and observational material.

Areas of interest are defined as issues of concern defined by the ASD individual, parents/caretakers, teachers, or other observers of the individual as requiring focus and attention in order to function more effectively in social interactions. Areas of interest may be concerning or problematic behaviors or interactions which would benefit from intervention. The Areas of Interest Form notes specific points that may be addressed in considering these issues. Attempts are made to categorize these points by their apparent importance, designating areas of interest as most significant, somewhat significant, or "other" significant. These categories are intended to facilitate translation into individual and group goals for the ASD individual. An area of interest is considered more significant (i.e., more important, more problematic) if it is noted by several observers and rated as less significant (i.e., less important, less problematic) if it is noted by fewer observers or observable only in certain defined, controlled situations. Some examples of general and specific "areas of interest" are provided in Appendix 1.

Figure 12.3 Social Competency and Social Skills Groups

Areas of Interest Form

Name: Grade:

Date of birth: School:

Age: City/Town:

Diagnosis:

Areas of interest:
- Issues of concern defined by ASD individual, parents, teachers, and/or observers
- Concerning or problematic behaviors or interactions noted by parents, teachers, and observers

Most significant overall areas of interest noted by (all): ASD individual, parents, teachers, observers

Other somewhat significant areas of interest noted by (two): ASD individual, parents, teachers, observers

Other less significant areas of interest noted by (any): ASD individual, parents, teachers, observers

Additional concerns noted:

Clinician name: Date:

Individual Goals Form (Figure 12.4)

This form is used to indicate specific goals based on areas of interest indicated by parent/caretakers, others working with the ASD individual, observers of the individual, and when appropriate, the ASD individual him/herself. It is the focus of this approach to create feasible goals for the ASD individual that can be worked on within the group-focused, peer-based, cognitive-developmental model presented here. As such, not all areas of interest, even when designated as most significant, may be chosen for translation into goals. This may occur when the designated area of interest cannot feasibly and appropriately be addressed within the group setting constructed. Some examples of individual goals constructed by specific stage are provided in Appendix 2.

Figure 12.4 Social Competency and Social Skills Groups

Individual Goals Form

Name: Grade:

Date of birth: School:

Age: City/Town:

Diagnosis:

Stage 1 Group formation and orientation goals:

Stage 2 Group cohesion goals:

Stage 3 Group stability, relationships, and connections goals:

Stage 4 Group adaptations and perspective taking goals:

Stage 5 Group termination, loss, and endings goals:

Additional concerns noted:

Clinician name: Date:

Group Goals Form (Figure 12.5)

Group goals are created by the group leaders based on the sets of individual goals for each ASD individual entering the group. Once the Individual Goals Form is completed and individual goals are constructed, then the goals for each ASD individual being considered for possible group placement are then aligned with other individuals being considered and emphasis is given to the "best fit" clustering within the group setting. Individual goals may be specific to the ASD individual, but must also be related to overall group goals. Attempts are made to maintain consistency and synergy between individual goals and group goals, but that is viewed from the larger perspective of the group as a whole. In other words, all individual goals must have some connection to a group goal and to a specific stage of group development with their attainment considered feasible within the overall approach described here.

Generally, these group goals will be specific to the whole group's needs and to the specific stage of group development within which they will be focused. Forward progression on group goals should coincide with individual goal attainment and will guide an understanding of the specific stage of group development that the group has achieved. Some examples of group goals constructed by specific stage are provided in Appendix 3.

Figure 12.5 Social Competency and Social Skills Groups

Group Goals Form

Group members: Grade range of group:

Age range of group:

Diagnoses of group members:

Stage 1 Group formation and orientation goals:

Stage 2 Group cohesion goals:

Stage 3 Group stability, relationships, and connections goals:

Stage 4 Group adaptations and perspective taking goals:

Stage 5 Group termination, loss, and endings goals:

Additional concerns noted:

Clinician name: Date:

Chapter 13

Introduction to a Stage Model of Group Development for ASD Individuals

Social competence and social skill training groups are constructed specifically to address the social interaction deficits exhibited by individuals with Autism Spectrum Disorders (ASD) within group settings. Within this approach, social competence groups emphasize the range of strengths and assets that ASD individuals bring to these situations as well as addressing directly the social interaction deficits exhibited. Through group-based intervention, the focus is placed on the following broad group goals:

1. Recognize and understand the complexity of social interchange and experience and understand what it means to be part of a group.

2. Manage group experiences, situations, and interactions effectively.

3. Emphasize and develop effective self-based functions, such as self-awareness, self-management, self-regulation, and insight, that are necessary for effective interpersonal and group interactions.

4. Develop and enhance the capacity to create and sustain meaningful interpersonal relationships with others, especially peers.

5. Address directly key issues which inhibit or prevent successful group interactions.

6. Learn and use consistently basic social skills necessary for successful social engagement.

To achieve these goals, a Process/Skill approach is employed. In this approach, process is defined as the functions or structures which underlie learning and that need to be experienced, learned, and actively engaged. Thus, in addressing process, key variables such as self-management, relatedness, attention, stress and anxiety management, flexibility, and perspective taking are taken into account and how these underlying process variables may be related to specific skills to be learned. A skill is defined as the actual tool or skill set necessary to complete a task, activity, or interaction in age appropriate, effective ways. The Process/Skill approach emphasizes an understanding of the underlying structures necessary to learn and perform skills related to group interaction. If the structures are present, then the skill can be taught and learned. If the structures are not present, emphasis must first be placed on developing and enhancing the appropriate structures, thus providing the capacity for the individual to subsequently learn the skills deemed necessary for the particular skill set.

In approaching social competence through the Process/Skill approach, a peer-based, group-focused, cognitive-developmental model is considered most effective in providing for the range of social-interactive needs demonstrated by ASD individuals.

General structure

Overall, this approach strongly endorses and employs structure and consistency within group situations with ASD individuals. This includes structure and consistency in: the placement of individuals within groups, the planning and constructing of individual and group goals, setting and maintaining a tone for each group session, allowing the flexibility and resiliency of the group flow to activate and play out when appropriate and useful to the group, using specific tasks and activities to emphasize a point and to learn specific skills, providing an environment for repetition and reinforcement of key process variables and learned skills, and creating an environment that allows the group to increasingly take ownership and responsibility for each step in the group development process. This approach includes structure and consistency within each weekly group that takes place as well as over the entire course of the year-long groups which extend to approximately thirty to forty sessions over the year.

Peer-based settings

In a social world, the skills needed to survive and flourish are varied and extensive. An understanding and awareness of the need and desire to connect, to relate, and to experience another individual in mutually reciprocal ways are necessary first steps.

Peer-based settings provide structured situations for these interactions to take place. They are purposefully constructed with consideration given to each individual's social competencies, developmental level, and emotional needs. They emphasize peer interactions over individual or group to adult interactions. They provide ongoing opportunities to engage peers, while at the same time, providing an understanding of an individual's own needs to acquire and develop underlying structures or key processes and to learn the specific skills for successful peer interaction. With increased individual self-skills (self-awareness, self-regulation, insight), group participants are encouraged and taught how to ally with and join their peers in the process of mutual and reciprocal interaction, negotiation, decision-making, and group reflection. While groups are initially adult-monitored so as to be structured to increase and positively reinforce mutual contacts, increasing responsibility is transferred gradually over the course of the group to peer members for the structuring of their own interactions in more effective ways as new and more complex social-interactive skills are learned and as new and more complex social-interactive situations are confronted.

Peer-based settings provide opportunities to experience others, to develop self-awareness of one's needs in these situations, and to consider how these needs can be responded to and met within peer-based interactions. Within peer-based settings, individuals are able to experience and understand the social rules and expectations which govern social interactions. They are able to learn and experiment with new ways to adapt to these interactions and to learn how to get their own needs met in these peer-based situations. Individuals must not only understand the rules and expectations of interaction (appropriate and inappropriate) and how they apply, but that these rules can be highly fluid and rapidly changing, based on a range of social, interactional, and contextual factors. Finally, peer-based settings allow individuals to exist within a group and to share their experiences with peers in a naturalistic setting that closely mirrors real life.

Group-focused settings

Membership in groups allows similar aged peers to come together for the common purposes of sharing experiences, learning from them, recognizing and addressing areas of social difficulty, and learning and practicing new skills to manage the social interactions which arise within a group more effectively. The experience of positive group membership has been consistently demonstrated to be a powerful force and contributing factor in influencing behavioral change, contributing to increased self-esteem, and building social-interactive skills (Yalom 2005).

Group interactions provide structured situations where individuals can interact with others with a focus on common issues and concerns while monitored by an adult facilitator and while working toward change and growth in specific, designated areas. These interactions provide opportunities for sharing of information, experiences, thoughts, and feelings. They allow for the establishment of co-operative, mutual, esteem-building, and often enduring relationships. They provide a setting for collaborative efforts directed toward individual and shared goals and they can provide opportunities for direct instruction and practice in needed skills to accomplish these group-based objectives. Group members become aware of and learn that the group process follows certain predictable patterns that can be anticipated, managed, and worked through, but that this group flow can also trigger concerns·and issues related to key variables and deficits, such as stress/anxiety, attention issues, inflexibility, narrowness of thinking, and even distortions. Since these are considered group issues, they are addressed through the group (e.g., group goals) and by group members as a group not as individuals.

Specific structure

With ASD individuals, consistent and predictable structures are necessary to establish a general sense of well being and to prepare an individual to manage the stress that will occur around interpersonal group interactions. Structured and consistent approaches to beginning each group appear necessary to allow the members to orient to the group, to facilitate transition from waiting room to group room, and to settle into the group process. Typically, each structured session begins with the group members to taking 3–4 minutes to orient to the group room with a controlled activity of their choosing, prior to coming to a table or common meeting area, typically in a circle, to convene the group. If the group is not able to manage this less structured transition, then a group transition activity is employed or an immediate convening of the group by the group leader occurs.

The group structure (used throughout the course of the group) typically requires that each child formally greet each other member of the group by name. The group leader initiates a brief period of general discussion, announcements, etc., which serves to reinforce and model the appropriate interaction process and to allow the group goals to be addressed and articulated as needed, then sorted out by the group for that specific session.

The group structure also includes a period of sharing of significant experiences, events, or interactions as designated by each group member, followed by a decision-making process of how the activities for that session will be selected based on group goals and the level of Stage 1 group formation and orientation process attained to that point.

In the early sessions, the group leader more actively directs these structures, but as the group forms and orients and moves to subsequent stages, the group itself is expected to assume the task of decision making and follow through. Therefore, initial groups are more highly structured, more group leader-directed, more focused on learning about one another and how to relate as a group, and more focused on defining an effective format for the group to proceed.

In later group sessions, the leader serves to guide the group through the structure set in place during early sessions. As the group practices and internalizes this structure, the leader becomes less active and directive, increasing expectations that group members self-initiate and move through the steps previously practiced. As the group matures, it will demonstrate its own areas of strengths and weaknesses as it struggles with leadership issues, decision making, task selection, conflict resolution, and follow through. Although the group leader becomes less active and directive as the group proceeds, depending on the group's capacities to self-manage, the leader maintains a primary role of facilitating key process and skill development through encouragement, constructive criticism, reinforcement, modeling, and identification.

As the group moves toward the final stages, the group leader ensures that needed issues are addressed, clarified, and processed as necessary. Thus, in these settings, the group structure provides the consistent foundation for the group to move from session to session, the group leader assures that the group develops the tools necessary for the group to move continuously forward, the group members provide power and energy (through bringing issues to the forefront) to address and confront interactional issues, and the group as a whole develops and exerts a stabilizing influence in keeping the group on course and working on its group goals toward a meaningful outcome.

Chapter 14

Stages of Group Development

Over the years in groups structured around social competence and social skill development, children have been observed moving through a series of stages during the course of both the short (6–8 weeks) and long-term (30 weeks) group programs. These stages follow a consistent sequence and appear related to specific processes, sets of skills, and modes of behaviors that occur at each stage and that are necessary to pass through the particular stage effectively in order to move forward and make use of subsequent stages.

The following stages are observed within these group interventions with ASD children:

Stage 1   Group Formation and Orientation

Stage 2   Group Cohesion

Stage 3   Group Stability, Relationships, and Connections

Stage 4   Group Adaptations and Perspective Taking

Stage 5   Terminations, Loss, and Goodbyes

Stage 1 Group Formation and Orientation

The stage of Group Formation and Orientation relates primarily to the task of several individuals coming together in the process of forming a group. This group will eventually develop a unique identity, a set of common goals, its own style of interaction, and its own set of group norms. During this first stage, the group leader takes a very active role in encouraging and facilitating opportunities, including the constructing of specific tasks and activities that foster sharing and learning about one another, especially around common interests. The group leader actively directs and guides discussion and activities that accentuate the interactive process during this stage.

This process of group formation includes establishment of group rules and expectations, dealing with stress and anxiety management, and making the group a structured, predictable, safe place where feelings and emotions can be expressed without attack, where resistance is addressed openly and directly, and where a sense of togetherness, connectedness, and community will develop and strengthen over the course of many group meetings. This stage relies heavily on the group leader's understanding of each individual's background and history, their areas of strengths and weakness, and multiple interrelated cognitive, behavioral, social, and emotional variables.

During the initial sessions, the group leader observes and attends to key behaviors with particular attention paid to information previously obtained during the application and interview phase and provided by parents and teachers relating to the group formation and orientation process. Group leader observations are then combined with the previously obtained information and with the set of individual "areas of interest" collected for each child prior to starting group to form individual goals for each group participant.

Individual's goals are constructed at the outset of Stage 1, particularly in the key process areas of stress-anxiety control and management, attention, and flexibility/transitions, based on the specific defined "areas of interest" indicated for each group member. As each child progresses through their individual goals and as the group moves through Stage 1 goals, then the group leader reviews current "areas of interest" for each child and constructs adjusted or modified individual goals for each child as needed as they move into Stage 2.

Group goals are also constructed at the outset of Stage 1 and are formed with an understanding of each group participant's individual goals. These individual goals are "pooled" to form more general group goals that will relate to the broader issues that the group as a whole will focus on. Group goals will also address as needed key process areas from this broader group goal perspective and will be reviewed frequently for adjustment and modification. These steps are repeated as the individual and group goals are met and as the group readies to move into each subsequent stage.

The initial stage of Group Formation and Orientation can last anywhere from one to two sessions to ten to twelve sessions. It is characterized by several key components which are translated into group goals. These goals are constructed with input from the group members and become the basis for structuring subsequent group activities.

Setting group goals for Stage 1

The group goals for Stage 1 Group Formation and Orientation will often include:

General
- building the group culture
- learning and practicing basic anxiety and stress reduction techniques
- encouraging members to actively attend to each other
- tolerating multiple kinds of input

Specific
- setting the rules
- defining the boundaries
- developing and describing this group's social code
- identifying with the group leader
- managing anxiety that arises around joining a group, meeting new people, sharing information about oneself
- paying attention to other members in the group
- giving everyone the opportunity to speak and to respond.

Group goals at Stage 1 focus on bringing the group members together, recognizing common areas of interest, and experiencing the normal tension and anxiety of being with others in goal-oriented, group situations. They are intended to provide structure about what is expected and what is and is not tolerated (e.g., setting and defining rules and boundaries), about what information, behaviors, thoughts, etc., fit within the group setting, and about shared feelings, thoughts, and experiences common to all group members when beginning in a new situation.

Group goals provide an overall focus on the common and shared experiences and needs of all group members, while individual "areas of interest" focus on specific concerns or behaviors that a particular group member may be working on. These may vary from one group member to another and will form the basis for constructing individual goals for each individual within the group. The group leader uses an individual's "areas of interest" and individual goals as guides for setting group goals (general and specific), for constructing the appropriate group structure, and for directing the selection of group tasks and activities at the specific stage.

Setting the group structure at Stage 1

The group structure at Stage 1 relates to the specific environment created and facilitated by the group leader together with the group members to enhance the building of a group culture and the establishment of a group identity. Discussions of group and individual goals result in the creation of the structure within which group members can function and within which these goals can be met. This relates to the building of a group culture wherein the group can effectively learn about one another, establish, understand, and follow, the rules it requires, and begin to test out the types of interaction it requires to function most effectively.

Gradually as the group moves through the stage of Group Formation and Orientation, members are able to demonstrate increased competency and mastery of these initial processes and as Stage 1 goals are achieved, the group is primed and prepared to move to Stage 2. Examples of this developing mastery include: the group entering the group room appropriately, being aware of and following group rules, and initiating and following through with group structures, such as directing themselves through group orienting activities, greetings, sharing, activity selection, and decision-making processes, all with reasonable success and minimal unresolved conflict.

One major issue with the great majority of ASD individuals which influences interactions at all stages, but particularly at Stage 1, relates to the experience and management of stress and anxiety. As described previously, the experience of stress, tension, and anxiety is prominent in nearly all interpersonal interactions with ASD individuals and therefore must be addressed and considered within each stage. At Stage 1, the management of stress and anxiety is specifically designated as one of the group goals so that it can be addressed and discussed directly from the outset of group. These initial discussions recognize that everyone will be "stressed and anxious" in beginning a new group and meeting new people. Therefore, the group will address this and learn to control it (a long term goal) by learning basic stress and anxiety reduction techniques (the short term goal).

Each initial group session and subsequent sessions in Stage 1 provide progressive and systematic training in simple stress and anxiety management techniques, such as deep breathing, rhythmic counting, and positive self-talk (as described briefly in Chapter Six), which are then repeated and practiced consistently within each Stage 1 session. This process also serves to trigger group discussions about what causes stress and anxiety, what it feels like, and what techniques or methods can assist in managing it, both adaptively and maladaptively. Most typically however, specific and more elaborate discussions of stress and anxiety occur at later stages. It should be emphasized here very strenuously the importance of recognizing and accommodating to the role that stress, tension, and anxiety play in social interactions with ASD individuals. Its emergence is inevitable, must be managed through awareness, consistent training and application of effective stress and anxiety reduction strategies, and acknowledged and managed throughout each stage of group development with ASD individuals.

A second major issue with ASD individuals which emerges early in Stage 1 and which is an issue to be addressed throughout each stage relates to attention. At each stage, depending on the group and individual needs, group goals are constructed around the development and enhancement of focused, sustained, selective, flexible, and joint attention. In particular in interpersonal, group settings, joint attention is an important and necessary competency for reciprocal interchange and communication. At Stage 1, each activity is constructed by the group leader to develop and reinforce joint attention among group participants. The group is primed in advance for the subsequent activities, with modeling, reinforcement, and stress management.

The third major issue which affects the majority of ASD individuals, particularly in interpersonal and group situations, relates to the issue of flexibility and transitions. The requirements to be flexible, adjust and accommodate to change, and to transition (i.e., shift attention) between tasks and activities are known to create significant degrees of stress and tension in the majority of ASD individuals, triggering increased stress, tension, and anxiety, and often overload (i.e., meltdown). Attempts are made to anticipate and prepare for the stress related to the needs for flexibility and transitions by discussing the issue with the group participants at Stage 1, by constructing group goals related to the issue, and by addressing the issue specifically (through modification of group goals and developing specific directed tasks and activities) at each of the five stages.

Specific skills to be addressed at Stage 1

Since Stage 1 relates to group formation and orientation, the specific skills addressed are those necessary for the initiation of a reciprocal relationship, including basic social interaction skills. These include basic interactive skills such as: eye contact, initiating a conversation, active listening, active responding, asking related and pertinent questions, and following directions.

When individuals within the group share common areas of interest or individual goals relating to any of these Stage 1 skills, then group goals are constructed and tasks and activities focusing on these skills are generated. See Appendix 4.1: Specific Skills Addressed at Stage 1.

Stage 2 Group Cohesion

The stage of Group Cohesion relates to the group's capacity to form a bond as a group and to use that bond as a force to hold the group together as it begins to deal with increasingly more stressful issues. The group leader has had the opportunity during Stage 1 to observe and influence how group members begin to connect as a group and to one another as individuals. Information learned about the group's strengths and weaknesses, particularly in the areas of stress-anxiety management, attention, and flexibility/transitions, will inform the construction of Stage 2 goals as the group moves forward.

Again as at Stage 1, information obtained during the application and interview process is reviewed by the group leader and combined with group observations in order to better understand how to foster improved communication and group identification and how to anticipate, based on previous information and current observations, where problems in social interaction will occur. In reviewing this information, additional areas of interest may be considered and included as the group proceeds to setting goals for Stage 2.

During this stage of group development, all activities, tasks, and communications are viewed through the lens of developing and solidifying the group as a cohesive, self-supportive unit. The group is encouraged to take more control (or as much as it can), particularly in participating in the setting of goals for the group, in decision-making procedures, and in fostering appropriate avenues for communication.

Setting group goals for Stage 2

The group goals for Stage 2 Group Cohesion will often include:

General
- developing and solidifying cohesion within the group and between group members

Specific
- the group jointly trying to set their own goals

- individual members identifying with the group

- establishing group communication methods

- requiring honesty/directness

- fostering reliance on one another

  managing stress and anxiety related to increased connectedness

- attention to active listening and active responding

- understanding and utilizing cooperative and flexible interactive strategies.

At Stage 2, group goals foster interaction, while individual goals work on specific aspects of a group member's thinking or behavior that will enhance group participation or that might interfere with effective group involvement. Group goals provide the opportunity for interaction, while individual goals focus on the specific needs of the individual to make interactions successful. For example, a Stage 2 group goal may focus on group decision making, while individual goals may focus on a member being more positive, using two different cooperation strategies, or going along with the majority.

As individual stage goals are met, the group goals take on greater significance as they begin to reflect more accurately the overall group process and progress. As specific group goals are met at Stage 2, group members are encouraged to begin to think about constructing group goals for Stage 3 Group Stability, Relationships, and Connections, a stage of increased group connectedness and independence.

There also is a continued emphasis on efforts to acknowledge, address, manage, and cope with the stress and anxiety that arises as individuals take risks to share personal information, join others in attempts to gain support and feedback, express needs that may feel personal and may be embarrassing, and recognize and express intimacy and affiliation needs. Following the learning and practicing of simple stress and anxiety reduction techniques learned in Stage 1, a broader forum for stress and anxiety control and management is now provided in Stage 2. This includes additional relaxation techniques, including the refinement of deep breathing, progressive muscle relaxation, positive self-talk, and visual imaging strategies, and extensive interactive discussion of "what works for you." Ongoing discussion and reinforcement of stress and anxiety reduction techniques play a key role in allowing Stage 2 Group Cohesion to take hold, flourish, and move toward Stage 3.

In addition, group members are pushed to develop or to enhance their capacities for joint attention, the process of "locking on" to another while speaking, listening, or connecting, as a means to facilitate relationship development and identify with other group members. Members are provided guidance in how to stay "tuned in," in how to follow conversational rules, and in how to become more self-aware of their own attentional style as it occurs within the group.

Group members are also provided strategies to assess their own capacities for flexibility, change, and transitions and to understand how these impact group connections and relationships. At Stage 2, group members are cued when flexibility issues arise, are encouraged to consider suggestions and alternative approaches, and are reinforced for appropriate responses to these situations.

Setting the Stage 2 group structure

The specific environment of Stage 2 relates to the group as a whole working together on common tasks directed toward common goals. In entering this stage, the group members have acquired significant information about one another and about their strengths and weaknesses and now have the capacity to use this information in both positive, growth-fostering, and negative, destructive, ways.

Information from prior parent and teacher data and current observations are used to develop goals for each individual and for the group, both generally and specifically focused on fostering cohesion through increased intermember and group communication, through identification with the group as whole as well as between individual members, and managing the tension/anxiety related to relationship building and the interactive process. Each individual is encouraged to generate specific individual goals for themselves that are linked to targeted group goals constructed with significant group involvement.

Specific skills to be addressed at Stage 2

Since Stage 2 Group Cohesion relates to developmentally more advanced usage of social competencies and social skills, those specific skills addressed represent more advanced use of skills learned at Stage 1, though still basic and necessary for common interactions. Stage 2 skills are those required to form relationships with others in basic and consistent ways. These include: initiating discussions of personal information and preferences, collecting and soliciting information about other group members including their interests and preferences, acknowledging points others make, sharing related information, regulating the intensity and quality of one's interactions (e.g., voice tone, voice volume, facial expressions, joint attention, body language and cues, etc.), and taking turns.

If individuals within the group share common areas of interest or individual goals relating to any of these Stage 2 skills, then group goals are constructed and tasks and activities focusing on these skills are generated. See Appendix 4.2: Specific Skills Addressed at Stage 2.

Stage 3 Group Stability, Relationships, and Connections

The stage of Group Stability, Relationships, and Connections emphasizes the real power of the interactive group process. The focus here is on tapping into the established and now ongoing stability that comes from the familiarity achieved between group members on rules, boundaries, and managing positive/negative interactions. Group members identify with other group members and with the group leader as strong alliances develop, but these relationships will vary between group members depending on the issue and the emotions connected.

Modes of communication are established, facilitated by the group leader, with significant emphasis placed on the development, enhancement, and reinforcement of positive modes and the diminishment and extinguishing of negative modes and styles of interaction. During this stage, the group must learn to directly and openly address and manage conflict and hostility when it arises between group members and to learn appropriate conflict resolution strategies.

At this stage, group members are expected to employ skills and strategies learned at previous stages to manage and deal with issues and concerns as they arise. A process of circular feedback is employed. When an issue arises and is managed by the group, these are then discussed and debriefed. When a similar issue arises at a later time, subsequent discussions and debriefings make explicit connections to the previous issues and manner of resolution, connecting the two and developing a series of possible solutions. The next time a similar issue arises, the group has been adequately primed to discuss and connect previous problem solving techniques to the current issue and to develop new solutions as needed. This pattern of circular feedback appears to be particularly effective with very verbal and articulate high functioning ASD groups.

Stage 3 provides a level of group stability and an opportunity to use meaningful and deepening relationships in group to solve issues. Connections in relationships are emphasized and connections of group experiences to real world, outside of group experiences are targeted and highlighted. As a group enters Stage 3, the opportunities for corrective group experiences occur with increasing frequency and the group leader must remain vigilant in pointing out, reinforcing, and using these situations to increase group awareness and insight.

Setting group goals for Stage 3

The group goals for Stage 3 Group Stability, Relationships, and Connections will often include:

General
- The group will take increasing control.

- Corrective experiences are provided and emphasized.

Specific
- Group members will help each other acknowledge and manage stress and anxiety when observed.

- Increased awareness and attention to the needs of others through feedback, support, and problem solving.

- Emphasis on flexible shifts requiring cooperative and interactive choices, problem solving, and decision making.

- The group will manage conflict and hostility as it arises.

- Modes of communication are defined and refined.

- Group acceptance and respect will emerge and solidify.

- The group will emphasize creating and maintaining memories of specific group situations and interchanges.

At this stage, the group is systematically encouraged to become more active in structuring the individual sessions based on a consensus of group needs. The group is positioned to initiate discussions, allocate time, resolve conflicts, respect and take care of one another, and continue to move forward on the discussed and articulated goals. The group leader increases the emphasis on his/her role as group facilitator and decreases emphasis on the role of decision maker for the group.

During Stage 3, the group goals focus on facilitating a gradual shift in the arrangement of power and control. The group as a whole will be required to discuss and understand the responsibility of taking on increasing power and authority in control, decision-making, and conflict resolution. By placing the emphasis on goals requiring communication enhancement, management of conflict and hostility, and acceptance of each group member as part of the group as a whole, the group is forced to address and sort out what is effective and constructive interaction and what is not in attempting to meet these goals.

Setting the Stage 3 group structure

The specific environment for Stage 3 relates to providing opportunities for the group to take control of managing issues, conflicts, communication, and aspects of decision making. The group setting is intended to encourage the taking on of this responsibility to manage the interactions and decisions on activity selection, time management, discussion, and free time and by emphasizing tasks and activities which gradually allow the group as a whole to assert itself as a decision-making force for its own benefit. The group leader gently moves the group though this stage, taking less and less of a controlling posture, and more and more that of an encouraging and supportive facilitator. By the end of Stage 3, the group leader smoothly moves back and forth from a facilitator to a consultant role.

With the increased responsibility taken on by the group as a whole, individuals speaking only for themselves have relatively little power unless they can garner group support. At this stage, even more vocal and assertive members are influenced and controlled by the joint efforts of the group with support by the group leader.

At Stage 3, the group also plays a significant role in influencing the type and intensity of stress and anxiety that emerges both for individuals and for the group as whole. For example, when a decision is made by the group to engage in a certain activity, an individual dissenter may experience increased stress and anxiety. At this stage, the group should have some awareness of the types of situations that trigger stress and tension in each of the group members and is encouraged to react to these events with responses that help the individual manage and control their level of stress and tension more effectively. At this stage, the group begins to demonstrate focused efforts to help one another manage and control stress and anxiety, to be sufficiently attentive to each members needs, and to join in making cooperative, flexible plans and decisions regarding what is in the group's best interests.

Specific skills to be addressed at Stage 3

Since Stage 3 relates to group stability, meaningful relationships, and solid connections, the specific skills addressed relate to maintenance of relationships in the "relationship zone," staying on topic and following changes in topic, cooperation, compromise, learning and understanding what makes a good friend, giving and receiving compliments.

If individuals within the group share common areas of interest or individual goals relating to any of these Stage 3 skills, then group goals are constructed and tasks and activities focusing on these skills are generated. See Appendix 4.3: Specific Skills Addressed at Stage 3.

Stage 4 Group Adaptation and Perspective Taking

The fourth stage of Group Adaptation and Perspective Taking relates to the group's capacity to adapt flexibly to a broad range of issues, behavior, and emotional reactions that may arise. This will include the ongoing positive and negative issues that arise each session as well as adjustments in time management, modes of communication, decision-making, and evaluating the needs of the group. As the issues or the group needs change or shift, the group must develop the capacity at this stage to adjust and adapt using the group interactions as the basis for the types of adaptations necessary.

During this stage, there is increasing emphasis on the goals of flexibility and ability to shift and on "theory of mind," that is, the capacity to think about and experience what another person might be thinking or feeling, i.e., "putting yourself in the other person's shoes." This emphasizes the need to understand situations and interactions, to recognize, experience, and feel the need for empathy toward others, and to respond accordingly.

Setting group goals for Stage 4

The group goals for Stage 4 Group Adaptations and Perspective Taking will often include:

General
- making necessary adaptations and adjustments
- responding with flexibility and the capacity to shift and change

Specific
- considering and using alternative approaches and views in decision making
- using assertiveness appropriately
- using feedback constructively
- repairing "breaks" in relationships
- living and surviving with disappointment
- experiencing empathy and responding appropriately.

At this stage, the group learns to manage and direct itself through the ups and downs of managing and resolving conflict, of repairing breaks in relationships, and of having to consider multiple points of view and alternative ways of thinking. The emphasis at this stage is on letting the group take increasing control, make decisions, resolve conflicts, adapt to change, and flexibly manage unknown or unpredictable situations.

The Stage 4 goals are constructed to ensure practice in self-management and self-direction by requiring honest and respectful interactions, appropriate confrontation, discussion of alternative solutions to problems, and unanimous agreement in decision making. Significant emphasis at Stage 4 is given to goals fostering flexibility, openness, and resiliency when faced with difficult, perplexing, and hard to solve problems. Activities are specifically constructed with these goals in mind.

Within Stage 4, the key variables and related goals for stress and anxiety control and management, joint attention, and flexibility and transitions, are now integrated within the discussions and interactions of the group and the weekly tasks and activities selected by the group. At this stage of group development, it is expected that group members have attained adequate levels of self-awareness and knowledge of their own stress and anxiety triggers both personally and occurring within the group context, can recognize and focus on the need for attention directed to the other group members across a variety of situations, and are able to tolerate the frequent shifts in group process that require flexibility and transition. At Stage 4, the group goals reflect this progression with stress and anxiety control and management and joint attention being thoroughly embedded within each group session. Group goals at this stage continue to emphasize flexibility and transitions as this remains a critical variable for the continuing development of group process variables and skills at the higher stages.

Setting the Stage 4 group structure

At this stage, the group demonstrates its capacity to appropriately take control and assert the competencies and the skills learned in previous stages. The group leader begins this stage in the role of facilitator and by the end of Stage 4 functions primarily as a consultant and observer to the group. The environment fostered is one of trust, support, flexibility, and encouragement of appropriate risk-taking. At this stage, the structure provided emphasizes the need and capacity to flexibly adjust and adapt to changing sets of information, interactions, and circumstances, with growing confidence that the group can manage unpredictable situations that they confront. As well, stress and anxiety producing personal and interpersonal situations can be managed effectively with stress and anxiety management techniques initiated on demand or prompted by peer pressure. Joint attention is recognized as necessary for effective interpersonal interaction and is engaged and maintained when appropriate for the situation.

Specific skills to be addressed at Stage 4

Since Stage 4 relates to group adaptations and perspective taking, the specific skills addressed at Stage 4 relate to flexibly adjusting to change, moving easily from one topic to another, agreeing to another's point of view, and negotiating or giving in to another's demands.

Stage 4 skills include: recognizing and interpreting nonverbal and conceptual cues, assertiveness, managing conflict and confrontation, giving and receiving criticism, using humor, role-playing, recognizing and using emotions in interactions, sympathy and empathy, and perspective taking.

If individuals within the group share common areas of interest or individual goals relating to any of these Stage 4 skills, then group goals are constructed and tasks and activities focusing on these skills are generated. See Appendix 4.4: Specific Skills Addressed at Stage 4.

Stage 5 Termination, Loss, and Endings

The Stage 5 Termination, Loss, and Endings relates to endings, losses, significant transitions, and goodbyes that occur within or related to the group. Attempts are made to understand the thoughts, feelings, emotions, and behaviors that these events stir up and the effects that they have on the interactions between group peers as well as on others outside of the group. This stage focuses on recognizing what these experiences are like, how to tell when they occur, and what effects they have on individuals. Typically, Stage 5 Terminations, Loss, and Endings begins when the end of group is announced or discussed with the end clearly in mind. In most of these groups, this begins 3–5 sessions prior to the last group session. It often includes heavily emotional discussions as endings stir up significant, often unresolved emotional content related to loss, transitions, and endings. Strong emphasis is placed on the need for the group leaders to prepare for this stage by constructing specific Stage 4 goals which facilitate the move into Stage 5 Termination, by setting a structure and environment which will manage and support the unpredictable emotional content, and by moving carefully and systematically into Stage 5.

Setting group goals for Stage 5

The group goals for Stage 5 Termination, Loss, and Endings will often include:

General
- addressing termination, loss, transition, change, and goodbyes

Specific
- recognizing termination feelings
- recognizing termination behaviors
- managing termination feelings and behaviors
- creating memories
- maintaining memories
- planning for goodbye
- saying goodbye.

The goals for Stage 5 Termination, Loss, and Endings focus on addressing and managing thoughts, feelings, emotions, and behaviors related to change, transitions, losses, and endings. Following the introduction of termination, the group members are encouraged and helped to create goals specific to endings. Here as in previous stages, the creating of individual goals should connect and relate to the overall group goals. The group members at Stage 5 should be able to agree on the appropriate construction of group goals and how these goals can be achieved within their group. Individual goals may more flexibly fit the individual group members needs and here too information and feedback from parent and teacher sources should be included as well as the group leader's observations of each individual's management of change, transition, loss, and endings within the group setting (i.e., as it relates to the individual's using other group members for support, security, etc.).

Setting the Stage 5 group structure

The Stage 5 group structure continues the themes of fostering emotional safety and security, redefining confidentiality and privacy issues, requiring openness and honesty between group members, encouraging the sharing of thoughts, feelings, and emotions, and tolerating flexibility in allowing for alternative ways of thinking and behaving. Over the course of moving through stages of group development, the group structure has very gradually reduced the amount of overall structure provided to the group in order to allow increased flexibility to develop and for the practice and use of learned skills around control, assertion, flexibility, and self-management to take place. The group as a whole is encouraged to self-direct discussions of issues related to endings as they arise. The group is expected to share relevant termination thoughts and emotions and to use their peers to process and understand these experiences. The group leader, as in previous stages, actively becomes less directive, more facilitative, and consultative, to the extent that the group can manage and tolerate.

Specific skills to be addressed at Stage 5

Since Stage 5 is about terminations, loss, and goodbyes, the specific skills addressed at Stage 5 relate to those thoughts, emotions, and behaviors related to endings of meaningful things in group members lives. These include saying goodbye, recognizing the loss associated with goodbyes, and creating a memory to preserve the relationship.

If individuals within the group share common areas of interest or individual goals relating to any of these Stage 5 skills, then group goals are constructed and tasks and activities focusing on these skills are generated. See Appendix 4.5: Specific Skills Addressed at Stage 5.

Specific skills related to stages of group development

Throughout the five stages of group development, primary consideration at each stage is given to the key variables necessary for relationship development of stress and anxiety control and management, joint attention, and flexibility and transitions. In providing training and practice in the development of specific skills, an ongoing awareness of the effects of these variables on the individual's capacity to learn and use skills is maintained. Training and practice of specific skills are constantly adjusted and modified based on the individual and group response to these underlying variables.

Over the past several years, with increasing interest in ASD, several programs have been developed addressing social skill development. Most programs attempt to follow a logical sequence paralleling normal social development and providing training and practice for social skills in a progressive and sequential manner. Many of these programs are well suited for use within the social skill development aspects of this approach with tasks and activities from these programs specifically selected and adapted for skill development at a particular stage.

Chapter 15

Roles that Individual Children May Take within the Group

The General

Typically, the individual who takes on the role of "The General" in a group situation is one who has a high need to be in control in most interpersonal situations. This often stems from a fear of losing control, a fear of being out of control, or a fear of having others in control (and not knowing what they will do or how they will act). This high need for control will also dictate the quality of this individual's interaction with others, that is, "The General" is in charge and he/she is likely to be intolerant of others who do not follow his/her orders, who argue or disagree with him/her, who try to assert their own views, who try to mediate for more moderate positions, or who side with others against him/her. In these situations, input or feedback from others, even from the group leader, is positioned so as to be of little value or useless.

In some situations to assure a position of control, "The General" will often appear to be "negotiating" with others, but in fact these are usually subtle or not so subtle forms of coercive techniques (e.g., "No, no, no, that won't work, we'll do it this way") intended to shift control back to "The General." These positions are not genuine or reciprocal and reflect an artificial "negotiating stance" or a resorting to "bribes" if in danger of losing control, often with no intention of following through on his/her promises or his/her end of the bargain. "Look, let's do this and next time, we'll do it your way." When the next time comes along, "The General" will anticipate the deal and likely undercut it with a series of alternative negotiations which are directed to keep "The General" in control and to render other's ideas or suggestions secondary to the will of "The General." In these situations, opposing views or information which disagree with his/her position must be recognized early and headed off before there can be any serious consideration of it or before it can take hold with one or more other group members.

"The General" may also use his/her position of control to "delegate," that is, he/she may allow others to make decisions through his/her authorizing authority (but only if he/she allows it) of this temporary shift of control. In fact, it is in reality, no shift in the control, only "The General" allowing a subordinate to share in his/her authority temporarily if followed through on "The General's" terms. Typically, if this appears to threaten "The General's" authority or control or appears to signal a shift away from "The General's" power and control, "The General" will initiate a battle to retain and win back the control of the group. Thus, others having any control or power must be contingent on "The General's" allowing it within his/her rules.

When there is another group member who will not back down from "The General" (and who may in fact be another "general" him/herself), then significant conflict, even chaos, is likely to break out. This arouses "The General's" fear of losing control represented by the other child's attempts to seize control, and must be thwarted, overcome, or undermined, often with ferocity, so that that the other child does not prevail and ultimately gain control, take the position of "The General," and subsequently dominate and control the former general.

✓

Figure 15.1 Suggested individual goals for "The General"

Stage 1	• The individual will learn to manage his/her stress and anxiety as it arises related to control issues. • The individual will recognize, but not hinder other's attempts to connect interpersonally within the group. • The individual will view the "group" as an entity and force.
Stage 2	• The individual will interact with peers respectfully and with interest in other's views. • The individual will respond positively to other's attempts to connect interpersonally. • The individual will recognize and acknowledge other member's needs for control.
Stage 3	• The individual will consider alternative views presented in group. • The individual will implement suggestions made by others on decision making or problem solving. • The individual will not resist or hinder other member's attempts to assert self or control aspects of group.
Stage 4	• The individual will alter own ways of thinking based on input from others. • The individual will acknowledge and encourage the need for other group members to share in control issues (i.e., decision making). • The individual will repair breaks in relationships that are self-created. • The individual will request points of view from other group members for group consideration.
Stage 5	• The individual will acknowledge his/her role within the group as "part of the group." • The individual will create termination memories about "the group." • The individual will acknowledge and recognize the importance of the "group," not one individual being in charge or in control.

The U.N. Observer

Typically, the child who takes on the role of "U.N. Observer" is one with low needs for control and in fact avoids situations where he/she will have control or have to make decisions. He/she is best characterized as a passive observer, willing to get involved only when the situation presents no risks or dangers to him/herself. Usually, this posture stems from a fear of not being cared for or of abandonment, that is, taking no risks assures that no rejection or abandonment will occur and supposedly that he/she will remain "liked/loved," taken care of, and an accepted part of the group.

"The U.N. Observer's" primary purpose is to avoid taking risks interpersonally. To accomplish this in a group, he/she tries to anticipate what others want him/her to do and in an attempt to keep others happy, he/she tries to be the compliant, easy to get along with peer. In order to avoid risks, the observer must take no strong or firm position, offer no opinions that deviate from the group norm, and take no clear sides in conflict. However, the avoidance of conflict is self-centered and self-protective, rather for the purpose of keeping calm for the sake of the group.

"The U.N. Observer" may take a role of mediator, but this most often occurs only when forced to by opposing group members. "The U.N. Observer," in this situation, will attempt to reflect or mirror both sides, but will rarely or overtly support one position or the other, letting the combatants do all the asserting and posturing for control. Needless to say, "The U.N. Observer" is reliant on others to take control, make decisions, and essentially dictate to him/her what he/she is to do. Ultimately, "The U.N. Observer" is forced to go along with the group norm or decision and to give up his/her own professed neutrality. This is solely in the service of allowing "The U.N. Observer" to remain passive and outside the realm of control. Only in this way can "The U.N. Observer" remain part of the group.

Although "The U.N. Observer" will avoid taking an active role in decision making, he/she is nevertheless likely to experience fairly high degrees of stress and anxiety. This relates to the uncertainty of their perceived role within the group and the possibility that the group could move quickly in one direction or another, leaving "The U.N. Observer" with no say or control over the outcome. The uncertainty of these situations appears to trigger high levels of stress and anxiety in "The U.N. Observer." Despite "The U.N. Observer's" refusal to take positions or to express opinions within the group, his/her greatest fear appears to be that he/she will in some way be left out of the group (e.g., rejected, abandoned). Thus, the role of neutrality and passivity in the face of conflict is intended to make him/her appear as valuable to either side of the conflict, willing to go along with either side, as long as the purpose is to eliminate the overt conflict, achieve a state of calm, and support the illusion of everyone getting along and agreeing.

In many situations, especially when recognizing the unpredictability of conflictual situations, "The U.N. Observer" will try to set the stage for calmness, serenity, and agreement (e.g., "Let's just do what we did last time"). "The U.N. Observer's" primary goal is to keep his/her own stress and anxiety in check by supporting the absence of conflict at best or the quick resolution of conflict at worst. For "The U.N. Observer," the absence of conflict maintains a state of "cautious contentment." This relates to his/her passive position that relies on the direction of others and on other's decision making. "The U.N. Observer" generally tends to absolve themselves through avoidance/denial of any responsibility for group behavior ("I didn't do anything, I just sat there and didn't say anything").

Figure 15.2 Suggested individual goals for "The U.N. Observer"

Stage 1	• The individual will recognize stress and anxiety related to asserting self and speaking up.
Stage 2	• The individual will offer their own suggestions, points of view, or opinions on group topics.
Stage 3	• The individual will assert self to have own suggestions, points of view, or opinions considered.
Stage 4	• The individual will assert self to have own suggestions, points of view, or opinions implemented.
Stage 5	• The individual will acknowledge and reflect upon learning to be active and to assert self within the group.

Forward Reconnaissance

Typically, the individual who takes on the role of "Forward Reconnaissance" (Recon) tends to be an individual who is very cautious, careful, and deliberate, although not usually viewed as passive, in most interpersonal relations. This individual appears to have capacities for delay, for anticipation of events and circumstances, to be risk avoidant, and to have moderate need for control. This individual likes the role of figuring out possibilities and being in a position of presenting his/her thoughts and points of view to the other group members.

The "Recon" seems to get his/her needs for control met by the process of collecting, understanding, and conveying the information collected, then trying to influence directly the direction of the decision making process. Though these individuals tend to be cautious and not individual risk-takers, he/she can easily join in a group risk-taking activity and get his/her energy directly from the group if he/she views the group as valuing their role as "Recon" and information gatherer. He/she will value feedback from others if this process allows them to maintain the role of "Recon," i.e., influence the decision/outcome, but he/she may also engage in manipulation of the flow of feedback if this process appears to be reducing or taking away control from him/her.

The "Recon" will often expend a fair amount of thinking about how different possibilities, alternatives, and choices may affect his/her own position as he/she lobbies for or attempts to direct a choice or decision. He/she will avoid getting in the middle of group conflicts, especially when over control or power, however, he/she may mediate differences and disputes, but will rarely take firm positions or sides, often giving what sounds like or appears to be "objective" views or opinions about the "best" way of proceeding. The "Recon" typically is aware of all the possible minefields ahead in a situation and attempts to avoid them personally or navigate around them interpersonally. His/her investment is in avoiding risk, conflict, and battle, while still being part of the group process, and getting something done.

Figure 15.3 Suggested individual goals for the "Forward Reconnaissance"

Stage 1	• The individual will recognize stress and anxiety related to uncertainty and unpredictability.
Stage 2	• The individual will acknowledge the support and connectedness from being part of a group.
Stage 3	• The individual will tolerate personal stress and anxiety and interpersonal unpredictability and conflict. • The individual will construct strategies to manage and cope with personal and interpersonal stress and anxiety to fit specific situations.
Stage 4	• The individual will allow problems and conflicts to emerge, to be "aired out," and to find solutions (i.e., the individual "trusts" the group to work it out). • The individual will self-initiate appropriate strategies to manage personal and interpersonal stress and anxiety when it arises.
Stage 5	• The individual will acknowledge and reflect upon needs for predictability within the group. • The individual will create memories-related uncertainty, variation, and unpredictability of this group (i.e., "I am OK with that").

The Mediator

Typically, this role is taken by the individual with high need for control, but who is conflict avoidant. He/she will relish the opportunity to be in control when in the middle of a conflictual situation as long as he/she is not a combatant. His/her need typically is to take control of the situation by influencing and directing the combatants. Ultimately, the direction of the resolution of group conflict is highly influenced by "The Mediator" and often it is his/her own way of thinking or point of view that ultimately prevails.

"The Mediator" often attempts to occupy the space between conflicting sides. He/she may collect information, explain the options, alternatives, or possibilities and appear to be actively seeking to find a middle ground. However, he/she is rarely satisfied with this role unless there is power and control attached to it and as long as it appears valued by the other group members.

"The Mediator" gains sustenance and energy from the importance and power that this role conveys, particularly in moving the group forward and not allowing the group to get stuck. "The Mediator" usually does not seek out or encourage conflict, but is quick to jump into the role of "Mediator" and to direct solutions. Generally, "The Mediator" is a risk-taker as long as this does not involve escalating conflict situations. Thus all control struggles within the group, often between two "Generals," are seen as opportunities for "The Mediator" to gain increased control by solving the emerging problem. The role of "The Mediator" allows the individual to be accepted and valued within the group.

Figure 15.4 Suggested individual goals for "The Mediator"

Stage 1	• The individual will recognize and tolerate the stress and anxiety of sitting, listening, and attending to others in the group. • The individual will attend to others when needs are being communicated and expressed.
Stage 2	• The individual will acknowledge contributions of every member as part of the group. • The individual will acknowledge and accept the central role of the group interactions.
Stage 3	• The individual will respect and accept the input of each group member as important. • The individual will refrain from "taking charge" behaviors or attempts to "force decisions." • The individual will acknowledge and accept the presence of conflict within the group.
Stage 4	• The individual will tolerate a range of different considerations, points of view, and opinions as part of group process. • The individual will tolerate other group members appropriately assuming problem-solving and decision-making roles within the group.
Stage 5	• The individual will reflect upon and relate memories regarding the group's need for differences, uncertainty, and unpredictability. • The individual will reflect upon and relate memories of how power and control is decided and delegated within the group and how problems and conflicts are resolved.

Chapter 16

Roles that the Group Leader May Take within the Group

The Expert

When the group leader assumes the role of the "Expert" in the group, he/she is making a statement that, "I am right, you are not!" That is, "What I say is the norm for the group based on my sole judgment." This position leaves little room for group input, group disagreement, or group negotiation. The message conveyed is, "I'm the only one who knows enough in this group to set rules, make decisions, give feedback, judge appropriateness," etc.

Often the group leader approaches this role with his/her own high needs for control and is attempting to assert him/herself in the role as leader. Although there are a number of aspects to this role that serve positive group leadership, generally, it tends to be a role that is overly rigid and restrictive with limited opportunities for the group members to gradually take on increased self-control and responsibility, to oppose structures in order to learn how to accommodate to them, and to observe models of flexible and supportive decision making and limit setting. Thus the group leader role of the "Expert" is best characterized as one of high control by the group leader, limited responsibility for the group members, and too narrow and rigid models for managing and responding to group issues and interactions.

Figure 16.1 Suggested goals for the group leader as "Expert"

Stage 1	• The leader intervenes only when rules are broken, boundaries exceeded, or respect violated.
Stage 2	• The group will be allowed to define aspects of their own identity to the extent that they are capable.
Stage 3	• The group will assume power and control in problem solving and decision-making to the extent they can manage.
Stage 4	• The leader acknowledges and accepts their role as facilitator-consultant within the group.
Stage 5	• The leader will reflect on the group's capacity and successes in self-managing and self-directing tasks and activities.

The Dictator

The group leader role of the "Dictator" is generally viewed as the counterpart to the authoritarian parent, but within the group setting. This is typically a role assumed by an adult who not only has high needs for control, but who has an inability to recognize the impact of these control needs as they play out in a group or to use them constructively in the service of positive interactions and outcomes. This is one of the primary negative leader roles because it provides so few opportunities (often none) for the group to generate any movement on issues such as testing group rules, discussing and trying out different variations of group structures, group decision-making, constructively altering the group dynamic, and providing feedback to the group leader and to other group members about different ways an issue or problem would be approached since the group leader dictates and rules on the right or wrong way to address an issue, carry out a command, interact with a peer, etc. (i.e., this is what you must do).

Since there is no flexibility tolerated by this therapist role, then the modeling effect generally tends to be pervasively negative and claustrophobic to the group members who may need to explore and experiment with different ways of addressing or approaching tasks, situations, or problems in order to grow and develop interpersonally.

Figure 16.2 Suggested goals for the group leader as "Dictator"

Stage 1	• The leader will encourage the group to consider and construct their own group rules defined by their own needs.
Stage 2	• The group leader will serve as guide and facilitator for task and activity selection. • The leader will encourage the group to design and construct their own task and activity selection schedule based on group goals
Stage 3	• The leader will encourage and facilitate the group to construct and devise problem-solving and conflict resolution strategies.
Stage 4	• The leader will allow the group to manage and resolve problems and conflicts as they arise in group.
Stage 5	• The group will reflect upon and recall effective self-directed and self-initiated problem-solving and conflict resolution strategies.

The Role Model

When the group leader assumes the role of the "Role Model," he/she is making a statement to the group members that you can follow my lead and do as I do without repercussion and with acceptance. It is a demonstration of how it can be done. "Try it, you'll like it." The group leader consciously acts out or demonstrates appropriate ways to interact and supportive things to say, using language and interactions that can be duplicated by the group members as is or reworked in their own language or style.

The group leader in the role of the "Role Model" sees him/herself as one who by demonstration provides the words, the acts, and the interactions not by talking about them, requesting they occur, or dictating that they be done, but by showing group members, by using the exact words, by using the exact tone, expression, and intonation, to get the point across.

The group leader as the "Role Model" typically exerts low needs for control as he/she relies on demonstration, repetition, and acceptance by the group. Rules are set and followed by demonstration and verbal "walk-throughs," such as "I am sitting quietly waiting for everyone's attention," "J. is ready and can begin." Those group members who comply by following the "Role Model" are provided with reinforcement and support, thus shaping the behavior to meet group norms. Reinforcement may be withheld from those who do not comply, but there are no negative consequences attached directly to the behaviors by the group leader.

The group leader as the "Role Model" typically assumes a nonjudgmental posture to inappropriate behavior by providing a description or demonstration of the desired appropriate behavior. Rather than setting strict verbal limits, such as "We don't use that language here," the group leader provides the appropriate modeled behavior, "We are all talking at the same time and cannot hear each other," "You're saying that J. hurt you and you're upset," or "We are excited and can't wait for vacation."

The group leader as "Role Model" establishes the rules and the behavioral norms by his/her modeling of the words, behavior, and interactions which provide an ongoing representation and demonstration of how appropriate interactions, verbalizations, and behaviors would sound and look like. The group members are encouraged through reinforcement to take on these demonstrations and verbalizations as their own, as appropriate ways to communicate with each other.

The Facilitator

The group leader as "Facilitator" conveys an image of control, structure, consistency, and goal directedness. The interactions of the "Facilitator" to the group are initially highly structured and provide the group with a series of connections throughout the course of the group. Initially, the connections relate to stage related issues, such as facilitating smooth and effective movement from one stage to the next. Other connections relate to the use of individual goals by each group member as they ally and connect with the group, followed by the discussion and development of group goals as they relate to individual issues.

The "Facilitator" provides the structure and consistency which encourages an inner sense of personal and group safety and security allowing individuals and the group to relate to one another in honest, respectful, caring, and empathic ways. Peer-based, therapeutic interactions evolve naturally in this environment. The "Facilitator" conveys a sense of control only when needed, leaving the group to struggle with its own self-management issues, to test their own limits, and when ready, to come up with their own mutually agreed upon solutions and decisions. The "Facilitator" allows the group to develop within their capabilities, tailored to individual and group needs, providing structure, consistency, and limits only when necessary to keep the group moving forward. The "Facilitator" moves from directing interactions, tasks, and activities, to facilitating their positive, stage-based movement, to observing the self-directed, self-managed, peer-based interactions of a cohesive and connected group.

Appendix 1: Examples of Areas of Interest

General

Always anxious/nervous (Stress/Anxiety management)

Never stops fidgeting (Stress/Anxiety management)

Will not try new things (Stress/Anxiety management, Flexibility)

Needs lots of preparation (Stress/Anxiety management, Flexibility)

Does not listen or pay attention (Attention)

Cannot stick with things/never finishes things (Sustained attention)

Ignores other people (Joint attention, Relatedness, Social-interpersonal, Peer relationships)

Avoids new things (Flexibility)

Always wants his/her own way (Flexibility)

Always has to win (Flexibility, Peer relationships, Theory of Mind)

Always late/hard to leave (Transitions)

Has no friends (Relatedness)

Cannot converse with peers (Relatedness)

Isolates self (Relatedness, Sensory)

Has temper tantrums (Self-control)

Will not acknowledge he/she is (upset, scared, angry, etc.) (Self-awareness, Emotional development)

Will not say how he/she feels (Self-awareness, Emotional development)

Wants friends (Peer relationships)

Says whatever he/she is thinking (Theory of Mind)

Specific

Does not look people in the eye (Joint attention)

Never says hello (Joint attention)

Does not respond to name when called (Attention)

Cannot wait for his/her turn (Attention, Self-control)

Blurts out (Attention, Self-control)

Does not follow rules (Flexibility)

Cannot agree with others (Flexibility)

Will not let others touch his/her things (Flexibility, Sensory)

Does not like (loud noises, yelling, getting touched, etc.) (Sensory)

Touches everything (Sensory)

Has no awareness of other's feelings (Theory of Mind)

Appendix 2: Examples of Individual Goals by Stage of Group Development

Stage 1

- I will introduce myself each time I meet someone new.
- I will say "hello" each time I see someone I know.
- I will ask an introductory question upon entering a conversation.
- I will initiate a discussion of a comfortable topic with a peer.

Stage 2

- I will ask how a peer is doing since last group.
- I will ask a question to a peer about something he/she mentioned at last group.
- I will ask a school-related question to a peer.
- I will ask a question relating to a peer's favorite… (hobby, activities, etc.).

Stage 3

- I will ask a peer for advice on something that I am interested in.
- I will ask a follow-up question related to a topic of a previous group.
- I will ask a "personal" question.
- I will share "personal" information with more than one peer and request input/advice.

Stage 4

- I will ask to help a peer on a personal topic raised by peer.

✓

- I will maintain appropriate interactive conversation throughout the group session.

- I will feel comfortable as a fully participating group member.

- I will ask the group for help with a "personal" issue or problem.

- I will acknowledge "feelings" about group participation.

Stage 5

- I will share my experiences as a group member.

- I will identify and label "feelings" related to ending group.

- I will acknowledge a "positive" and a "negative" group experience.

- I will learn about how I say goodbye to this group.

Appendix 3: Examples of Group Goals by Stage of Group Development

Stage 1

- The group will acknowledge the stress and anxiety of beginning a new group.
- The group will learn everyone's favorites (food, TV show, computer game, etc.).
- The group will learn about and acknowledge common interests.
- The group will self-initiate hellos, sharing, and activity suggestions.
- The group will discuss and understand the use of group rules and expectations.

Stage 2

- The group will self-initiate interactive discussions.
- The group will share individual choices for group decision making.
- The group will establish a "communication system" for the group.
- The group will acknowledge and understand the need for and use of "respect."

Stage 3

- The group will provide input/advice upon individual request.
- The group will consistently interact on all issues with "respect" for one another.
- The group will recognize issues of "conflict" as they arise.
- The group will recognize the needs of others and consider responses.

Stage 4

- The group will recognize and provide "help" to others spontaneously and without request.

- The group will resolve issues of group conflict.

- The group will spontaneously support one another when in need.

- The group will confront group members who deviate from group rules and expectations.

Stage 5

- The group will acknowledge, address, and support shared stress/anxiety around ending group.

- The group will self-initiate discussions of "group memories."

- The group will self-initiate end of group activities (party, memory book, etc.).

- The group will acknowledge, discuss, and support each other's end of group "feelings."

- The group will discuss other non-group endings and relate them to this group experience.

Appendix 4.1: Specific Skills Addressed at Stage 1

Entering a group

Introductions of self

Initiating a conversation:

- Eye contact

- Opening comments

- Facial expressions

Maintaining a conversation (Conversational skills):

- Active listening

- Active responding

- Asking related and pertinent questions

- Staying on topic

- Waiting

Expressing interest in others

Following directions

Exiting a group:

- Ending a conversation

- Saying goodbye

Appendix 4.2: Specific Skills Addressed at Stage 2

Initiating discussions using personal information and preferences

Soliciting personal information from others

Sharing personal information relevant to the topic or discussion

Taking turns in conversation

Taking turns in activities, tasks, or games

Acknowledging points/information that others contribute

Playing by the rules

Asking for help

Regulating the intensity and quality of one's interactions

Voice tone/voice volume

Facial expressions

Joint attention

Body language/body cues

Appendix 4.3: Specific Skills Addressed at Stage 3

Understanding and respecting body space

Sharing (of things that matter to the individual)

Cooperation

Helping one another

Compromise

Giving and receiving compliments

Giving encouragement

Expressing feelings

Assertiveness

Disagreeing

Being a good sport

Following changes in topic

Friendship:

- Discussing and understanding what is a friend
- Discussing and understanding what is a friendship
- Discussing and understanding what is a good friend

Discussing and understanding who is not a friend

Confronting teasing, putdowns, or bullying in a group

Understanding and using verbal interchanges:

- Reading verbal signals
- Reading nonverbal signals

Appendix 4.4: Specific Skills Addressed at Stage 4

Recognizing and interpreting nonverbal and conceptual cues

Assertiveness

Offering an opinion or suggestion

Giving and receiving criticism

Asking permission

Apologizing

Using humor

Role-playing

Introduction of others

Recognizing and using emotions in interactions

Perspective taking

Sympathy and empathy

Managing conflict and confrontation:

- Initiating discussion of conflict and confrontation
- Responding to conflict and confrontation

Discussing and resolving decision-making issues

Discussing and resolving problem-solving issues

✓

Appendix 4.5: Specific Skills Addressed at Stage 5

Recognizing the loss associated with goodbyes

Expressing the loss associated with goodbyes

Recognizing the feelings and emotions associated with goodbyes

Experiencing the feelings and emotions associated with goodbyes

Creating memories to preserve the relationships

Celebrating the loss, termination, or goodbyes

Saving the loss, termination, or goodbyes

Saying goodbyes

References

Alexander, F.G. and Selesnick, S.T. (1966) *The History of Psychiatry.* New York: Harper and Row.

American Psychiatric Association (1980) *Diagnostic and Statistical Manual for Mental Disorders,* 3rd edition. Washington, DC: American Psychiatric Association.

American Psychiatric Association (1987) *Diagnostic and Statistical Manual for Mental Disorders,* 3rd edition revised. Washington, DC: American Psychiatric Association.

American Psychiatric Association (1994) *Diagnostic and Statistical Manual for Mental Disorders,* 4th edition. Washington, DC: American Psychiatric Association.

Asperger, H. (1979) "Problems of infantile autism." *Communication: Journal of the National Autistic Society* 13, 45–52.

Asperger, H. (1991) [1944] "Autistic Psychopathy in Childhood." In U. Frith (ed.) *Autism and Asperger Syndrome.* Cambridge: Cambridge University Press.

Attwood, T. (2007) *The Complete Guide to Asperger's Syndrome.* London: Jessica Kingsley Publishers.

Axline, V. (1964) "The Eight Basic Principles." In M. Haworth (ed.) *Child Psychotherapy: Practice and Theory.* New York: Basic Books.

Barry, T.D., Klinger, L.G., Lee, J.M., Palardy, N., Gilmore, T., and Bodin, S.D. (2003) "Examining the effectiveness of an outpatient clinic-based social skills group for high functioning children with autism." *Journal of Autism and Developmental Disorders 33,* 6, 685–701.

Bauminger, N., Schulman, C., and Agam, G. (2003) "Peer interaction and loneliness in high-functioning children with autism." *Journal of Autism and Developmental Disorders 33,* 5, 489–507.

Bender, L. (1952) *Child Psychiatric Techniques.* Springfield, IL: Charles C. Thomas.

Berger, H.J.C., van Spaendonck, K.P.M., Horstinck, M.W., Baylenhuij, E.L., Lammers, P.W. and Cools, A.R. (1993) "Cognitive shifting as a predictor of progress in social understanding in high functioning adolescents with autism: A prospective study." *Journal of Autism and Developmental Disorders* 23, 341–359.

Bernet, W. and Dulcan, M.K. (2007) "Practice parameters for the assessment and treatment of children, adolescents, and adults with autism and other pervasive developmental disorders." *Journal of the American Academy of Child and Adolescent Psychiatry 38,* 12, 32S–54S.

Bleuler, E. (1951) [1916] "Lehrbuch der Psychiatrie." In A.A. Brill (trans.) *Textbook of Psychiatry.* New York: Dover.

Bourne, E.J. (2005) *The Anxiety and Phobia Workbook,* 4th edition. Oakland, CA: New Harbinger Publications.

Bowlby, J. (1952) *Maternal Care and Mental Health.* Geneva: World Health Organization.

Brown, B.B., Hedlinger, T., and Mieling, G. (1995) "The power in universality of experience: A homogeneous group approach to social skills training for individuals with learning disabilities." *Journal for Specialists in Group Work 20*, 98–107.

Caplan, G. (1955) *Emotional Problems of Early Childhood*. New York: Basic Books.

Cautela, J.R. and Groden, J. (1978) *Relaxation: A Comprehensive Manual for Adults, Children, and Children with Special Needs*. Champaign, Il: Research Press.

Centers for Disease Control and Prevention (2007) *Prevalence of Autism Spectrum Disorders in Multiple Areas of the United States, Surveillance Years 2000 and 2002*. Surveillance Summaries, February 9, 2007. Accessed on 23/09/07 at www.cdc.gov.

Center for Environmental Health, Environmental Epidemiology Program (2005) *Prevalence Estimates of Autism and Autism Spectrum Disorder in Massachusetts. Final Report*. Boston: Massachusetts Department of Public Health.

Charlop-Christy, M.H. and Kelso, S.E. (2003) "Teaching children with autism conversational speech using a cue card/written script program." *Education and Treatment of Children 26*, 108–128.

Ciesielski, K.T., Courchesne, E., and Elmasian, R. (1990) "Effects of focused selective attention tasks on event-related potentials in autistic and normal individuals." *Electroencephalography and Clinical Neurophysiology 75*, 207–220.

Clarke-Stewart, A. and Koch, J.B. (1983) *Children: Development through Adolescence*. New York: Wiley and Sons.

Courchesne, E. (1991) "Neuroanatomic imaging in autism." *Pediatrics 87*, 5, 781–790.

Davis, M., Eshelman, E.R., and McKay, M. (2000) *The Relaxation Response and Stress Reduction Workbook*, 5th Edition. Oakland, CA: New Harbinger Publications.

Dawson, G. (1991) "A Psychobiological Perspective on the Early Socio-Emotional Development of Children with Autism." In D. Cicchetti and S.L. Toth (eds) *Rochester Symposium on Developmental Psychopathology: Vol. 3. Models and Integrations*. Rochester, NY: University of Rochester Press.

Dawson, G. and Lewy, A. (1989) "Arousal, Attention, and the Socio-Emotional Impairments of Individuals with Autism." In G. Dawson (ed.) *Autism: Nature, Diagnosis, and Treatment*. New York: Guilford Press.

Dawson, G., Meltzoff, A.N., Osterling, J., Rinaldi, J., and Brown, E. (1998) "Children with autism fail to orient to naturally occurring social stimuli." *Journal of Autism and Developmental Disorders 28*, 479–485.

Delis, D.C., Kaplan, E., and Kramer, J. (1999) *Delis-Kaplan Executive Function System Manual*. San Antonio, TX: Psychological Corporation.

DeMyer, M., Hingtgen, J., and Jackson, R. (1981) "Infantile autism reviewed: A decade of research." *Schizophrenic Bulletin 7*, 388–451.

Dettmer, S., Simpson, R.I., Myles, B.S., and Ganz, J.B. (2000) "The use of visual supports to facilitate transitions of students with autism." *Focus on Autism and Other Developmental Disabilities 15*, 163–169.

Ehlers, S., and Gillberg, C. (1993) "The epidemiology of Asperger syndrome. A total population study." *Journal of Child Psychology and Psychiatry 34*, 8, 1327–1350.

Ferguson, A., Ashbaugh, R., O'Reilly, S. and McLaughlin, T.F. (2004) "Using prompt training and reinforcement to reduce transition times in a transitional kindergarten program for students with severe behavior disabilities." *Child and Family Behavior Therapy 26*, 17–24.

Flannery, K.B. and Horner, R.H. (1994) "The relationship between predictability and problem behavior for students with severe disabilities." *Journal of Behavioral Education 4*, 157–176.

Fombonne, E. (2003) "Epidemiological surveys of autism and other Pervasive Developmental Disorders: An update." *Journal of Autism and Developmental Disorders 33*, 4, 365–382.

Frith, U. (1989) *Autism: Explaining the Enigma.* Oxford: Basil Blackwell.

Frith, U. (1991) "Asperger and his Syndrome." In U. Frith (ed.) *Autism and Asperger Syndrome.* Cambridge: Cambridge University Press.

Frith, U. and Baron-Cohen, S. (1987) "Perception in Autistic Children." In D.J. Cohen, A. Donnellan, and R. Paul (eds) *Handbook of Autism and Pervasive Developmental Disorders.* New York: Wiley.

Ghaziuddin, M., Ghaziuddin, N., and Greden, J. (2002) "Depression in persons with autism: Implications for research and clinical care." *Journal of Autism and Developmental Disorders 32*, 4, 299–306.

Ghaziuddin, M., Leininger, L., and Tsai, L. (1995) "Brief report: Thought disorder in Asperger syndrome: Comparison with high-functioning autism." *Journal of Autism and Developmental Disorders 25*, 3, 311–317.

Gillberg, C. (1983) "Perceptual, motor, and attentional deficits in Swedish primary school children: Some child psychiatric aspects." *Journal of Child Psychology and Psychiatry 24*, 377–403.

Gillberg, C. (1991) "Clinical and neurobiological aspects of Asperger syndrome in six family studies." In U. Frith (ed.) *Autism and Asperger Syndrome.* Cambridge: Cambridge University Press.

Gillberg, C. and Gillberg, I.C. (1989) "Asperger syndrome – some epidemiological considerations: A research note." *Journal of Child Psychology and Psychiatry 30*, 631–638.

Gray, C. (1998) "Social stories 101." *The Morning News 10*, 1, 2–6.

Gray, C. (2000) *The New Social Stories Book.* Arlington, TX: Future Horizons.

Gumpel, T. (1994) "Social competence and social skills training for persons with mental retardation: An expansion of a behavioral paradigm." *Education and Training in* Mental *Retardation and Developmental Disabilities 29*, 3, 194–201.

Haworth, M. (ed.) (1964) *Child Psychotherapy: Practice and Theory.* New York: Basic Books.

Helmstetter, S. (1987) *The Self-Talk Solution.* New York: Pocket Books.

Jacobsen, P. (2003) *Asperger Syndrome and Psychotherapy: Understanding Asperger Perspectives.* London: Jessica Kingsley Publishers.

Jacobson, E. (1974) *Progressive Relaxation.* Chicago: University of Chicago Press.

Kadesjo, B., Gillberg, C., and Hagberg, B. (1999) "Autism and Asperger syndrome in seven-year-old children: A total population study." *Journal of Autism and Developmental Disorders 29*, 327–331.

Kanner, L. (1957) *Child Psychiatry,* 3rd edition. Springfield, IL: Charles C. Thomas.

Kanner, L. (1958) *In Defense of Mothers,* 4th edition. Springfield, IL: Charles C. Thomas.

Kanner, L. (1973) [1943] "Autistic Disturbances of Affective Contact." In L. Kanner (ed.) *Childhood Psychosis: Initial Studies and New Insights.* Washington, DC: V.H. Winston. (Original work published in *The Nervous Child,* 1943.)

Kanner, L. and Eisenberg, L. (1956) "Early infantile autism." *American Journal of Orthopsychiatry 26*, 55–65.

Kern, L. and Vorndran, C.M. (2000) "Functional assessment and intervention for transition difficulties." *Journal of the Association for Persons with Severe Handicaps 25*, 212–216.

Kinsbourne, M. (1987) "Cerebral Brainstem Relations in Infantile Autism." In E. Schopler and G.B. Mesibov (eds) *Neurobiological Issues in Autism.* New York: Plenum Press.

Klein, G.S. (1970) *Perception, Motives, and Personality.* New York: Knopf.

Klein, M. (1954) "Psychoanalysis of Children." In E. Jones (ed.), J. Strachey (trans.) *International Psychoanalytic Library.* London: Hogarth Press.

Klin, A., Jones, W., Schultz, R., Volkmar, F., and Cohen, D. (2002) "Defining and quantifying the social phenotype in autism." *American Journal of Psychiatry 159*, 6, 895–908.

Klin, A. and Volkmar, F.R. (2000) "Treatment and Intervention Guidelines for Individuals with Asperger's Syndrome." In A. Klin, F.R. Volkmar, and S.S. Sparrow (eds) *Asperger Syndrome*. New York: Guilford Press.

Koegel, R.L. and Frea, W.D. (1993) "Treatment of social behavior in autism through the modification of pivotal social skills." *Journal of Applied Behavior Analysis 26*, 369–377.

Lazarus, R.S. and Folkman, S. (1984) *Stress, Appraisal, and Coping*. New York: Springer.

Leekham, S., Libby, S., Wing, L., Gould, J., and Gillberg, C. (2000) "Comparison of ICD-10 and Gillberg's criteria for Asperger syndrome." *Autism 4*, 11–28.

Lezak, M.D. (1995) *Neuropsychological Assessment* 3rd Edition. Oxford: Oxford University Press.

Lovaas, O.I., Koegel, R.L., and Schreibman, L. (1979) "Stimulus overselectivity in Autism: A review of research." *Psychological Bulletin 86*, 1236–1254.

Lovaas, O.I., Young, D.B., and Newsom, C.D. (1978) "Childhood Psychosis: Behavioral Treatment." In B. Wolman, J. Egan and A.O. Ross (eds) *Handbook of Treatment of Mental Disorders in Childhood and Adolescence*. Englewood Cliffs, NJ: Prentice-Hall.

Loveland, K.A. and Landry, S.H. (1986) "Joint attention and language in autism and developmental language delay." *Journal of Autism and Developmental Disorders 16*, 335–349.

Mahler, M.S. (1952) "On Child Psychosis and Schizophrenia: Autistic and Symbiotic Child Psychosis." *Psychoanalytic Study of the Child*, vol. 7. New York: International Universities Press.

Mahler, M.S. (1968) *On Human Symbiosis and the Vicissitudes of Individuation. Vol. I, Infantile Psychosis*. New York: International Universities Press.

McEvoy, R.E., Roger, S.J., and Pennington, B.F. (1993) "Executive function and social communication deficits in young autistic children." *Journal of Child Psychology and Psychiatry and Allied Disciplines 34*, 563–578.

Mirsky, A.F., Anthony, B.J., Duncan, C.C., Ahearn, M.B., and Kellam, S.G. (1991) "Analysis of the elements of attention: A neuropsychological approach." *Neuropsychology Review 2*, 109–145.

Mishna, F. and Muskat, B. (1998) "Group therapy for boys with features of Asperger syndrome and concurrent learning disabilities: Finding a peer group." *Journal of Child and Adolescent Group Therapy 8*, 3, 97–114.

Nevin, J.A. (1996) "The momentum of compliance." *Journal of Applied Behavior Analysis 29*, 535–547.

Odom, S.L. and McConnell, S.R. (1985) "A performance-based conceptualization of social competence of handicapped preschool children: Implications for assessment." *Topics in Early Childhood Special Education 4*, 1–19.

Ornitz, E.M. (1989) "Autism at the Interface Between Sensory and Information Processing." In G. Dawson (ed.) *Autism: Nature, Diagnosis, and Treatment*. New York: Guilford Press.

Pierce, K.L., Glad, K., and Schreibman, L. (1997) "Social perception in children with autism: An attentional deficit." *Journal of Autism and Developmental Disorders 27*, 3, 261–278.

Pierce, K.L. and Schreibman, L. (1995) "Increasing complex social behaviors in children with autism: Effects of peer implemented pivotal response training," *Journal of Applied Behavior Analysis 28*, 285–295.

Pierce, K.L. and Schreibman, L. (1997) "Using peer trainers to promote social behavior in autism: Are they effective at enhancing multiple social modalities?" *Focus on Autism and Other Developmental Disabilities 12*, 207–218.

Ray, K.P., Skinner, C.H., and Watson, T.S. (1999) "Transferring stimulus control via momentum to increase compliance in a student with autism: A demonstration of collaborative consultation." *School Psychology Review* 28, 622–628.

Repp, A.C. and Karsh, K.G. (1994) "Hypothesis-based intervention for tantrum behaviors of persons with developmental disabilities in school settings." *Journal of Applied Behavioral Analysis 27*, 21–31.

Rie, H.E. (1971) "Historical Perspectives of Concepts in Child Psychopathology." In H.E. Rie (ed.) *Perspectives in Child Psychopathology*. Chicago: Aldine-Atherton.

Romano, J.P. and Roll, D. (2000) "Expanding the utility of behavioral momentum for youth with developmental disabilities." *Behavioral Interventions 15*, 99–111.

Rosenn, D. (2002) "Is it Asperger's or ADHD?" (*AANE*) *Asperger's Association of New England News 10* , 3–5.

Santangelo, S.L. and Tsatsanis, K. (2005) "What is known about autism: Genes, brain, and behavior." A*merican Journal of Pharmacogenomics, 5*, 71–92.

Scattone, D., Tingstrom, D.H., and Wilczynski, S.M. (2006) "Increasing appropriate social interactions of children with autism spectrum disorders using Social Stories." *Focus on Autism and Other Developmental Disabilities 21*, 4, 211–222.

Schatz, A.M., Weimer, A.K., and Trauner, D.A. (2002) "Brief report: Attention differences in Asperger syndrome." *Journal of Autism and Developmental Disorders 32*, 4, 333–336.

Schmit, J., Alper, S., Raschke, D., and Ryndak, D. (2000) "Effects of using a photographic cueing package during routine school transitions with a child who has autism." *Mental Retardation 38*, 131–137.

Schreibman, L., Whalen, C., and Stahmer, A.C. (2000) "The use of video priming to reduce disruptive transition behavior in children with autism." *Journal of Positive Behavior Interventions 2*, 3–11.

Selye, H. (1993) "History of the Stress Concept." In L. Goldberger and S. Breznitz (eds) Handbook of Stress: Theoretical and Clinical Aspects, 2nd Edition. New York: Free Press.

Shores, R.L. (1987) "Overview of research on social interaction: A historical and personal perspective." *Behavior Disorders 12*, 233–241.

Sigman, M., Mundy, P., Sherman, T., and Ungerer, J. (1986) "Social interactions of autistic, mentally retarded, and normal children and their caregivers." *Journal of Child Psychology and Psychiatry 27*, 647–656.

Singer, G.H., Singer, J., and Horner, R.H. (1987) "Using pretask requests to increase the probability of compliance for students with severe disabilities." *Journal of the Association for Persons with Severe Handicaps 12*, 287–291.

Sterling-Turner, H.E. and Jordan, S.S. (2007) "Interventions addressing transition difficulties for individuals with autism." *Psychology in the Schools 44*, 7, 681–690.

Stevens, S. and Gruzelier, J. (1984) "Electrodermal activity to auditory stimuli in autistic, retarded, and normal children." *Journal of Autism and Developmental Disorders 14*, 245–260.

Suldo, S.M., Shaunessy, E. and Hardesty, R. (2008) "Relationships among stress, coping, and mental health in high-achieving high school students." *Psychology in the Schools 45*, 4, 273–290.

Szatmari, P. (1991) "Asperger's syndrome: Diagnosis, treatment, and outcome." *Psychiatric Clinics of North America 14*, 81–93.

Szatmari, P., Brenner, R., and Nagy, J. (1989) "Asperger's syndrome: A review of clinical features." *Canadian Journal of Psychiatry 34*, 554–560.

Tustin, R.D. (1995) "The effects of advance notice of activity transitions on stereotypic behavior." *Journal of Applied Behavior Analysis 28*, 91–92.

Volden, J. and Johnston, J. (1999) "Cognitive scripts in autistic children and adolescents." *Journal of Autism and Developmental Disorders 29*, 3, 203–211.

Volkmar, F.R., Lord, C., Bailey, A., Schultz, R.T., and Klin, A. (2004) "Autism and pervasive developmental disorders." *Journal of Child Psychology and Psychiatry 41*, 135–170.

Wilczynski, S.M., Menousek, K., Hunter, M., and Mudgal, D. (2007) "Individualized education programs for youth with Autism Spectrum Disorders." *Psychology in the Schools 44*, 7, 653–666.

Wing, L. (1981) "Asperger's Syndrome: A clinical account." *Psychological Medicine 11*, 115–130.

Wing, L. (1988) "The Continuum of Autistic Characteristics." In E. Schopler and G. Mesibov (eds) *Diagnosis and Assessment in Autism*. New York: Plenum.

Wing, L. (1991) "The Relationship between Asperger's Syndrome and Kanner's Autism." In U. Frith (ed.) *Autism and Asperger Syndrome*. Cambridge: Cambridge University Press.

Wing, L. and Gould, J. (1979) "Severe impairments of social interaction and associated abnormalities in children: Epidemiology and classification." *Journal of Autism and Developmental Disorders 9*, 11–29.

World Health Organization (1978) *International Classification of Diseases, 9th Edition*. Geneva: World Health Organization.

World Health Organization (1993) *International Classification of Diseases, 10th Edition*. Geneva: World Health Organization.

Yalom, I.D. (2005) *The Theory and Practice of Group Psychotherapy, 5th Edition*. New York: Basic Books.

Subject Index

Author Index